Cox on

THE BATTLE FOR

the English

Curriculum

Brian Cox

Hodder & Stoughton

A MEMBER OF THE HODDER HEADLINE GROUP

For Three Wise Women

whose names appear often in these pages:

Joan Clanchy
Professor Katharine Perera
Professor Bridie Raban-Bisby

British Library Cataloguing in Publication Data

A catalogue record for this title is available from the British Library

ISBN 0 340 63938 5

First published 1995
Impression number 10 9 8 7 6 5 4 3 2 1
Year   1999 1998 1997 1996 1995

Typeset by Multiplex Techniques, Orpington, Kent.
Printed in Great Britain for Hodder & Stoughton Educational, a division of Hodder Headline Plc, 338 Euston Road, London NW1 3BH, by Athenaeum Press, Gateshead, Tyne and Wear.

Contents

National Curriculum English, 1989
Six controversies
     Speaking and Listening. Knowledge about Language.
     Grammar. Standard English. Creative writing.
     Multicultural education.
Changes in teaching English since the 1960s
     Rules of language. Coursework. The canon.
LINC: Language in the National Curriculum

An interview for NCC
Takeover at NCC and SEAC
Political control of the curriculum
Rhetoric of the Right
Standards
Prince Charles

Acknowledgment

I am most grateful to many people who have read portions of this manuscript, and given advice, particularly Cary Bazalgette, Professor Ronald Carter, Mrs Joan Clanchy, Graham Frater, Bethan Marshall, Professor Katharine Perera and Professor Bridie Raban-Bisby. I am also grateful to the many teachers, advisers and inspectors I met during the period covered by this book and with whom I discussed the English National Curriculum. My book includes many quotations from such people which were of great benefit to me when I was involved in disputes in newspapers and on radio and television. Those whose conversation or speeches or writings I found particularly helpful include Beverly Anderson, Pat Baldry, Michael Barber, Anne Barnes, Pat Barrett, Myra Barrs, Bob Bibby, Malcolm Bradbury, Gillian Brown, Marilyn Butler, John Carey, Urszula Clark, Trevor Dickinson, Annabelle Dixon, Henrietta Dombey, Sally Feldman, James Fenton, Terry Furlong, Rex Gibson, Duncan Graham, Sue Hackman, Peter Harding, John Hickman, Alan Howarth, Ted Hughes, Jeff Hynds, Lisa Jardine, John Johnson, Michael Jones, Bill Laar, Mike Lloyd, Colin MacCabe, Beverley Naidoo, Sibani Raychaudhuri, John Richmond, Michael Rosen, Peter Thomas, Jeremy Treglown, Shona Walton and Alastair West.

I am especially grateful to Patricia Rowan, the Editor of the *Times Educational Supplement*, who invited me to participate in the 'Shakespeare in the Curriculum' debate in the Royalty Theatre in London in 1992; to Cary Bazalgette and Patricia Rowan who invited me to participate as a witness at the Commission of Inquiry into English at the National Film Theatre in November 1993; to the members of NATE, LATE and NAAE, who gave me several opportunities to address their conferences; and to Channel 4, which gave me 26 minutes of prime time in the *Opinions* series to air my views on English and the National Curriculum. I should also like to thank the many people who invited me to lecture and gave me their views at so many welcome repasts, including Paul Foot who invited me to a *Private Eye* lunch in Soho and Lord Brian Griffiths who proved he was willing to listen and argue over lunch at the Garrick. I am grateful to Sir Ron Dearing, who gave me an hour of his time when he was very busy.

I should like to record again my appreciation of the support I received from the National Curriculum English Working Group, which was responsible for what is called the Cox Report of 1989: Mrs Di Billups, Ms Linda Cookson, Professor Katharine Perera, Roger Samways,

Professor David Skilton, Brian Slough, Professor Michael Stubbs and Dr Charles Suckling. The effect of their work continues, and after the battles from 1991 to 1995 must remain an essential text for all discussions of programmes of study for English in schools.

Extracts from consultation documents and the successive versions of the English National Curriculum are Crown copyright – see Select Bibliography.

The structure of the English curriculum

The 1995 English curriculum Order includes a useful Foreword with information about the framework of the National Curriculum. The main details which are relevant to English and the matters raised in this book are as follows:

The National Curriculum applies to pupils of compulsory school age in maintained schools, including grant-maintained and grant-maintained special schools. It is organised on the basis of four Key Stages which are broadly as follows:

	Pupils' ages	Year groups
Key Stage 1	5–7	1–2
Key Stage 2	7–11	3–6
Key Stage 3	11–14	7–9
Key Stage 4	14–16	10–11

For each subject and for each Key Stage, the National Curriculum puts forward Programmes of Study which set out what pupils should be taught and Attainment Targets which set out the expected standards of pupils' performance.

At the end of Key Stages 1, 2 and 3, standards of pupils' performance are set out in eight Level Descriptions of increasing difficulty, with an additional description above level 8 for exceptional performance. At Key Stage 4 public examinations are the main means of assessing attainment in the National Curriculum. New GCSE syllabuses which reflect the revised National Curriculum will be introduced for courses beginning in September 1996.

The revised Programmes of Study and Attainment Targets for English came into effect on 1 August 1995 for all year groups in Key Stages 1, 2 and 3. They come into effect on 1 August 1996 for Year 10 in Key Stage 4, and on 1 August 1997 for Year 11 in Key Stage 4.

Chronology of main events

1974	The Bullock Report, *A Language for Life*.
1976	James Callaghan, Labour Prime Minister, makes his Ruskin College speech, calling for a 'great debate' on education.
1979	Conservatives under Margaret Thatcher win General Election.
1984	HMI's *English from 5 to 16* proposes learning objectives for children at ages seven, eleven and sixteen, under the headings Listening, Speaking, Reading, Writing and Knowledge about Language.
1986	Kenneth Baker succeeds Sir Keith Joseph as Secretary of State for Education.
July 1987	DES issues *The National Curriculum 5–16: A Consultation Document* which announces a ten-subject national curriculum for England and Wales which is to be 'broad and balanced'. English, Maths and Science will be the core subjects.
Dec 1987	The Task Group on Assessment and Testing under the chairmanship of Professor Paul Black produces recommendations for assessment, including a ten-level scale for measuring pupil achievement.
1988	The Kingman Report: Committee of Inquiry into the Teaching of English Language puts forward a model of the English language in use, and makes recommendations for the teaching of knowledge about language in teacher training programmes.
1988	Education Reform Act establishes the National Curriculum Council (NCC, chaired by Duncan Graham), the Curriculum Council for Wales (CCW) and the School Examinations and Assessment Council (SEAC, chaired by Philip Halsey).
April 1989	Language in the National Curriculum (LINC) project set up to follow the implications of the Kingman Report and develop teaching materials to improve learning about language.
June 1989	Cox National Curriculum Working Group for English Report, *English for Ages 5–16*.
July 1989	John MacGregor succeeds Kenneth Baker as Secretary of State for Education.
March 1990	DES publishes Statutory Order, *English in the National Curriculum*, to be phased into schools over years 1990–4.
Nov 1990	Kenneth Clarke succeeds John MacGregor as Secretary of State for Education.
June 1991	LINC teaching materials withheld from publication by Tim Eggar (Minister of State).
Aug 1991	Duncan Graham at NCC is replaced by David Pascall, and Philip Halsey at SEAC is replaced by Lord Brian Griffiths.

Jan 1992	The DES Discussion Paper, *Curriculum Organisation and Classroom Practice in Primary Schools*, by Robin Alexander, Jim Rose and Chris Woodhead (the 'three wise men'), argues that effective delivery of the National Curriculum requires a mixture of teaching methods.
March 1992	Education (Schools) Act reduces numbers of HMI and reconstitutes them to form the new Office for Standards in Education (OFSTED).
April 1992	Conservatives under John Major win General Election.
April 1992	John Patten becomes Secretary of State for Education.
July 1992	NCC publishes *National Curriculum English: The Case for Revising the Order*, arguing that the English Curriculum needs to be defined more precisely.
1993	SEAC publishes Key Stage 3 English Anthology.
April 1993	DFE issues proposals for revision of National Curriculum English in *English for Ages 5–16 (1993)*.
April 1993	Sir Ron Dearing appointed as chair-designate of new School Curriculum and Assessment Authority (SCAA) and commissioned to review the National Curriculum and assessment arrangements.
May 1993	Widespread boycott of the Key Stage 3 English tests for fourteen-year-olds.
July 1993	Education Act 1993 establishes SCAA to replace NCC and SEAC.
Aug 1993	Sir Ron Dearing's Interim Report.
Sept 1993	NCC publishes *Consultation Report* on proposals for revision of English.
Nov 1993	British Film Institute Commission of Inquiry into English.
Dec 1993	Final Dearing Report, *The National Curriculum and its Assessment*.
1994	SCAA publishes *Evaluation of the Implementation of English in the National Curriculum at Key Stages 1, 2 and 3 (1991–1993)* (The Warwick Report).
May 1994	SCAA publishes *English in the National Curriculum: Draft Proposals*.
July 1994	Gillian Shephard replaces John Patten as Secretary of State for Education.
Jan 1995	DFE publishes *English in the National Curriculum*, for implementation from September 1995.

Introduction

Autumn 1995 confronted teachers with a new, slimmed-down English curriculum, presenting new opportunities and new problems. It is generally agreed among teachers that the new English curriculum lacks vision. It reduces the curriculum to basics, many of which are cliches, and at the same time it includes some confusions and falsities of emphasis which I examine later in this book. Both pupils and teachers in the slimmed-down curriculum are to some extent reduced to technicians, and the joy and wonder of the subject are lost. On the other hand, the 1995 English curriculum is superior to the drafts of a revised English curriculum which were proposed in 1993. Many absurdities have been removed, and the new curriculum gives teachers some freedoms to develop their own programmes of work.

In an article in the *Times Educational Supplement (TES)* on 2 December 1994, Nicholas Tate, Chief Executive of the School Curriculum and Assessment Authority (SCAA), explained that the aim of the new curriculum was to promote the basics of literacy and numeracy. Priority for the basics was a key feature of the review of the whole curriculum undertaken by Sir Ron Dearing in the summer of 1993. The purpose of the review, Tate explained, was not to provide 'vision', but to slim down an overloaded curriculum. No new content was to be added: '*the purpose was to refine the National Curriculum to a statement of the minimum which by law must be taught, and to provide a broad statutory framework within which schools could create and pursue their own vision.*'

SCAA sees the new National Curriculum as a pile of building bricks which can be assembled in a variety of ways to construct edifices of different kinds. The review brought a new flexibility, with 20 per cent of 'free time' in Key Stages 1 to 3, rising to 40 per cent at Key Stage 4. At every Key Stage, there is greater freedom within subjects to exemplify broad principles in different ways, and to treat some topics in outline and others in depth. Tate looks forward to further discussions about this arrangement, which he says were previously inhibited by an overloaded national curriculum.

This flexibility is good news, but teachers must worry about how this new policy will translate itself into assessment. The danger of an English curriculum devoted to basics is that testing will also be reduced to basics, and that teachers will be forced to teach to the tests, particularly if their future careers depend to some extent on their schools' position in league tables. This problem crops up repeatedly in my account of the arguments about the English curriculum. The battle to bring into being a proper, enriching assessment policy will surely be waged from 1996 onwards for many years to come.

In the meantime the great battle from 1991 to 1995 for control of the English curriculum has resulted in this slimmed-down, uninspiring curriculum. Millions of pounds have been wasted. The 1989 English National Curriculum set up by my Working Group was thought by teachers to provide for the teaching of English language and literature a coherent framework which reflected what the best teachers were already doing in their classrooms. My Working Group included teachers of high quality and leading professionals in the study of English teaching. Professor Katharine Perera, now Pro-Vice-Chancellor at Manchester University, combined considerable teaching experience in the classroom with an international reputation for research. Graham Frater, adviser to my Working Group, was chief HMI for English. In this book I quote at length their reactions to the disastrous attempts to rewrite the English curriculum. The quality of their contributions contrasts markedly with the mistakes and naiveties endemic in the revised versions.

For the many reasons set out in this book, I urge that the 1989 English curriculum should remain the teaching blueprint for teachers of English: **the 1995 curriculum does not prevent this**. The 1989 curriculum was not perfect, and in my third chapter I deal with some deficiencies and problems revealed by the Warwick research. Teachers at individual schools need to develop their own programmes of study based on good practice and what is best for children, not on arid prescriptions from government. I hope this book will help teachers to understand what went wrong after 1991, to develop coherent policies for an English curriculum, to understand what the new National Curriculum demands (and what it leaves unsaid), and to rediscover commitment and vision.

The Cox Report:
Context and Aftermath

National Curriculum English, 1989

I chaired the National Curriculum English Working Group whose
Report was submitted to Mr Kenneth Baker, Conservative Secretary of
State for Education, in May 1989. The Programmes of Study were
introduced into the classroom for five-year-olds in the autumn of 1989
and for eleven-year-olds in 1990. Some changes were made by the
National Curriculum Council (NCC) as a result of the consultation
process, but these were not substantial. My book, *Cox on Cox: An English
Curriculum for the 1990s*, gives full details of this curriculum, plus an
account of the political context in which it was prepared.

The 1989 English curriculum was given statutory force by parliament
for all children from the ages of five to sixteen in state schools in
England and Wales. In 1992 NCC decided to revise the 1989 English
Order. After several drafts and periods of consultation a new Order was
published in 1995 intended to provide stability by being left unchanged
for five years. This book describes the reception of the 1989 curriculum,
the arguments for and against revision, the political pressures from 1991
to 1995, and the virtues and defects of the new slimmed-down English
curriculum which was introduced into schools in autumn 1995.

The 1989 English curriculum (often popularly called the Cox
Report) combined the best of traditional and progressive approaches to
education. The 1980s witnessed a growing consensus about good
practice in the classroom, and this was reflected in our Report. We

divided the curriculum into five attainment targets: Speaking and Listening, Reading, Writing, Spelling and Handwriting. The 1995 English curriculum keeps this arrangement, except that there is now only one attainment target for Writing, and this incorporates the previous attainment targets for Spelling and Handwriting.

The 1989 English curriculum was received with enthusiasm by a large majority of teachers. In a 1993 poll of teachers conducted by the National Union of Teachers, almost 90 per cent said they thought there was no need to change the present curriculum arrangements. Unfortunately this curriculum received a mixed and muddled reception from the press. On the front cover of *Cox on Cox* we printed contradictory headlines. On the one side we have: '*Victory to Baker: Kenneth Baker has won his battle to make sure that all pupils leave school with a firm grasp of grammar and Standard English.*' This is set alongside: '*Baker accepts defeat on teaching of grammar: Mr Kenneth Baker, the Education Secretary, yesterday conceded that the government cannot force schools to adopt his preference for formal grammar teaching.*' The newspapers could not come to terms with the complex arguments in the Cox Report on how to teach grammar and Standard English, and they simplified according to their prejudices.

For months after the publication of the Cox Report I lectured at conferences, published essays in newspapers and books, and gave numerous interviews on radio and television to explain that the Cox Report strongly advocated the teaching of grammar and Standard English, not by old-fashioned rote learning and mechanical exercises, but by introducing pupils to new, stimulating classroom programmes of study on knowledge about language. *Cox on Cox*, which was published in 1991, includes chapters explaining our rationale. The 1989 curriculum gives due weight to spelling and grammar, but, instead of tedious drill, children are encouraged to write their own stories, to discuss them with the teacher and their friends, and to improve them, perhaps for printing in a class or school magazine. In their discussions with the teacher, grammar and knowledge about language can be introduced to help children improve their writing skills. It does not help much to make a child learn off by heart that a verb is a 'doing' word. The verb '*to be*' is not. What is needed is for children to understand how they can communicate more forcefully if they use active verbs. Teachers were excited by these new approaches to language, and found them of great help in teaching children of all abilities.

Unfortunately a small group of traditionalists, mainly associated with the right-wing Centre for Policy Studies and pressure groups such as the

Campaign for Real Education and the Queen's English Society, mounted a vigorous campaign against the Cox Report, and their writings and speeches were often reported in the press. These groups wanted an increased use of phonics in the teaching of reading, old-fashioned grammar lessons, the imposition of what was called 'grammatically correct spoken Standard English' for all children from the age of five, and lists of prescribed classics from English literature. Their belief in a standardised language together with their reverence for Shakespeare show how little they understand about the extraordinary vitality of Shakespeare's language. Yet in 1991 this group took control of the National Curriculum – see chapter 2.

Teachers welcomed the tone in which the Cox Report was presented, its emphasis on entitlement for pupils rather than prescription, on learning rather than instruction, because this reflected what was best about approaches to English teaching over the previous twenty years or so. The new curriculum of 1989 talked about opportunities for pupils, and did not adopt a rigid, authoritarian stance. As a result its opponents often accused the Cox Report of being 'woolly' – of not being sufficiently precise and prescriptive, for example, about the grammatical terms to be learnt by children. But our emphasis on entitlement and learning accompanied a robust demand for high standards in terms of content. Indeed, in terms of content (ie the knowledge, skills and understanding required) the Cox Report is more rigorous and demanding than any official document published at least since 1945. The following list of our recommendations shows that we demanded more than was customary in the 1980s in large numbers of primary and secondary schools:

◆ We introduced the systematic teaching and assessment of **spelling**.
◆ We required the teaching of both printed and cursive **handwriting** styles (previously many children had been allowed to devise their own way of producing letter shapes).
◆ We introduced the systematic teaching of **punctuation**, with the allocation to levels of full stops, question marks, exclamation marks, inverted commas, commas, apostrophes, semi-colons, and colons. Our requirement that some full stops and capital letters should be used accurately by level 2 (top infants) came much earlier than was widely the case in 1989.
◆ We required that a *range* of types of **writing** should be taught throughout the school years and from the earliest stages. In the 1970s and 1980s many schools concentrated on 'creative' writing, particularly on stories to the virtual exclusion of transactional types of writing.

◆ We put forward an explicit policy, related to stage and level, with regard to the expectation of **Standard English** in writing. Our requirement that it be expected by level 4 (top juniors) was very much earlier than some influential educationalists have advocated. Some have argued that written Standard English should not be required until the two years preceding public examinations at the age of sixteen.

◆ We required that pupils should **speak** audibly and intelligibly to a range of audiences, small and large, known and unknown.

◆ Pupils were required to speak Standard English by level 7. This is very difficult for pupils who do not speak Standard English at home, and some teachers felt this recommendation was too demanding.

◆ We said children should read works not written specifically for children in order to reach level 6, and should read pre-twentieth century works in a range of genres in order to reach level 7. We did not impose a prescribed canon, except that **Shakespeare** was made compulsory, but allowed teachers to choose pre-1900 texts they felt their children might enjoy. In schools in the 1970s and 1980s many children read post-war novels almost exclusively, with perhaps the occasional Liverpool poet thrown in.

◆ We introduced systematic and explicit teaching about the **forms and functions of language**. Our programmes of study were intended to arouse an enthusiastic interest in language, including grammar.

That this tough regime was accepted with enthusiasm by teachers is very much to their credit. From 1989 to 1991, when the traditionalists took over the National Curriculum, it was generally agreed that standards were improving.

When in 1992 the NCC published *National Curriculum English: The Case for Revising the Order,* teachers were astonished at its misrepresentations of the 1989 curriculum. I examine this document in detail in chapter 4.

Six controversies

In the final chapter of *Cox on Cox* I listed six areas in which the 1989 Report was controversial: speaking and listening, knowledge about language, grammar, Standard English, creative writing and multicultural education. These controversial proposals reflected changing attitudes to

English teaching which were anathema to old-fashioned traditionalists nostalgic for the school-rooms of the 1930s.

Speaking and Listening

Dr Marenbon, the traditionalist who after the 1991 shake-up became Chair of the English Group of the School Examinations and Assessment Council (SEAC), argues that speaking and listening should not be part of a national curriculum. This view was also held by his wife, Dr Sheila Lawlor, Deputy Director of the right-wing think tank, the Centre for Policy Studies, which was set up by the late Lord Joseph in the 1970s. In the *Observer* of 22 December 1991, Sheila Lawlor was reported as saying that

❝ at the moment there is great stress on 'speaking' and 'listening'. We doubt that that should be part of the syllabus at all. Nor should 'role play' and much of the drama that takes place. There is nothing wrong with any of these things, but they take time away from the essentials.

In contrast, my Working Group allocated one-third of the weighting in the assessment process to speaking and listening, thus altering the balance of English teaching away from exclusive concentration on reading and writing.

During the consultation exercise, the business community supported this new emphasis on high standards of speaking and listening, for communication in the modern world increasingly depends on effective speech. Terry Furlong, recently Chair of the National Association of Teachers of English (NATE), tells how a conference of business people was asked, if only one subject were prescribed for a national curriculum, what should this be? They chose Drama. Role play is now a common feature of business training. The subject of Drama, of course, also includes the precise use of expository prose in the analysis of plays, as well as cooperation and leadership of a group involved in producing a play. *Cox on Cox* explains why drama activities increasingly play a vital role in lessons in both primary and secondary schools.

Knowledge about Language

Our recommendations concerning knowledge about language (KAL) – severely cut in the NCC revised drafts of 1993 - were meant to increase understanding of the varieties of English, and so promote tolerance between different language groups. In *Cox on Cox* I wrote: '*Pupils should be helped to understand that clear, accurate English is of vital importance, but also that Standard English is not a form fixed immutably for eternity, but changes slightly from decade to decade.'* After the 1989 curriculum was published, teachers found that children can become fascinated by language change. As a man in his mid-sixties, I might say: '*I motored to the aerodrome with my wife listening to the wireless.*' Three words here – '*motored*', '*aerodrome*' and '*wireless*' – are no longer in common usage among young people. Recently when I used this example in a lecture, an undergraduate pointed out to me that '*wife*' too is out-of-date. I should have said '*partner*'. After 1989 publishers brought out lively textbooks on knowledge about language which were starting to revolutionise English language teaching. Children were encouraged to understand the importance of Standard English, yet also to appreciate the status of dialect and to value the richness of those other languages which in our multicultural society many children speak at home.

Grammar

When I was at school in the 1930s and 1940s English was often taught badly. After the outbreak of war in 1939 the Army found that many conscripts were illiterate, and could not read firearm and safety instructions. In those years children were taught rules about the English language which are now recognised as false. A teacher in his mid-fifties told me that when he was at school he was cuffed for writing 'a dilapidated wooden shed'. ' "*Lapis*" means a stone,' proclaimed his teacher, tweaking his ear. 'You foolish boy; you can't call something wooden dilapidated.' As late as the 1960s a professor at Bedford College told his students that 'companion' must be used only for a person with whom one eats ('panis' means 'with bread, food'). These teachers were applying Latin rules to English, and we now realise that this is ridiculous. Children were taught not to begin sentences with 'and' or 'but', and not to end a sentence with a preposition. They were told not to split the infinitive. For many years now linguists have been demonstrating that these rules do not apply to the English language.

Great writers such as Byron and D.H. Lawrence split their infinitives. The excellent Reader's Digest *The Right Word at the Right Time* (1986) says that the rule that you must not split the infinitive is 'irrational'. Phrases such as '*to boldly go where no man has gone before*' and '*begin to silently hope*' are guaranteed to set the pedant's teeth on edge, despite the greater regularity of 'to boldly go' or 'to silently hope'. In a witty entry in his *A Dictionary of Modern English Usage* (revised by Gowers, 1965), H. W. Fowler pokes fun at those pedants whose tortuous efforts to avoid split infinitives are deaf to the normal rhythms of English sentences. Particularly in speech we all (even the Prime Minister) continually split infinitives. This does not mean that standards are in decline, for often, particularly in spoken forms, a split infinitive gives extra vitality. In some usages, such as '*I try to really help my students*', the split infinitive provides an implication which is changed if 'really' is put before or after. Children enjoy playing games with words, and can improve their use of language when they study the various reasons for splitting or not splitting the infinitive.

Older people get very upset when they are told that the English rules they were taught at school are wrong. The way we write and speak is part of our identity, and it is destabilising to find that modern usage has left us behind. This is why many elderly traditionalists become so emotional about language. Some of these were placed in charge of National Curriculum English in 1991.

Lay people often believe that grammatical exercises should be imposed on all pupils, and that this would improve standards of writing. They are unaware that there is a considerable body of research which shows this is not the case. The formal teaching of grammar refers to systematic instruction in the analysis of sentences. It is systematic in the sense that it is deliberately designed to help students break down sentences into their component parts. It includes instruction on the labelling of sentence components – subject and predicate, phrases, clauses, word classes (nouns, verbs, prepositions) – and their use in breaking down, building up and editing sentences. This kind of teaching was common in the 1930s when I was at school.

Many pieces of research have shown that these grammatical exercises do not raise standards. Among the most important was a New Zealand study carried out between 1970 and 1973 (W.B. Elley *et al.* 1975: 'The Role of Grammar in a Secondary School Curriculum' in *New Zealand Journal of Educational Studies, 10,* pp. 26–42; reprinted in *Research in the Teaching of English,* 10, pp. 5–21). The language growth of 248 pupils in eight matched classes from a large suburban co-educational high school was monitored over three years. One group studied a traditional grammar course, one a transformational grammar course, and the third had no grammar teaching at all. Reviewing the evidence at the end of three years, the researchers concluded that '*it is difficult to escape the conclusion that English grammar, whether traditional or transformational, has virtually no influence on the language growth of typical secondary school students.*' The problem with research into the teaching of grammar (or into the teaching of reading) is that it is easy to cite small-scale projects based on one or two schools and a few teachers that show some method of teaching raises standards. New methods of teaching, whether traditional or progressive, often raise standards because the teachers engage in the novel project with added enthusiasm and determination. The New Zealand project is of great significance because it was large-scale, and because its findings reflect those of other large-scale projects in other parts of the world in the 1960s and 1970s.

In the 1950s and 1960s good teachers started rejecting exercises in grammar because they clearly were not raising standards. Unfortunately some of them went to the other extreme. The pendulum swung too far. Because grammar had been taught badly, they taught no grammar. 'Creative' writing became fashionable, and in some classrooms children were encouraged to express themselves freely without bothering about spelling, punctuation and grammar.

The Cox Report strongly opposed this trend, and recommended carefully structured programmes of work based on language in use. We urged that grammatical terminology should be introduced as a common vocabulary for teachers and pupils to discuss their own writing. Our proposals for knowledge about language were intended as a major pedagogical experiment which would need careful evaluation. Government interference since 1991 has considerably undermined this experiment, and, in my view, damaged the improved standards in literacy which are likely when pupils become fascinated by language in use.

A fierce debate about grammar took place immediately after the Cox Report was published. In the Winter 1990 issue of *Critical Quarterly* Colin MacCabe called this media furore over grammar the most ignorant and the most viciously stupid public debate of the past twenty years. The Kingman Inquiry into the teaching of English language (1988) rejected a return to the formal teaching of a grammar derived from Latin which was customary in most schools before 1960. At the same time it insisted that for children not to be taught *anything* about language is seriously to their disadvantage. Our Report followed this approach, arguing that all children are entitled to receive systematic and explicit teaching about the forms and functions of language. We said that children should understand the grammatical rules of Standard English, or language in use, and that they should be able to speak and write Standard English in appropriate contexts.

Standard English

I have already described our recommendations for written Standard English. We had major problems with spoken Standard English, and our explanations were often misrepresented in the press by journalists who wanted children to speak 'correctly'. We said that dialects should be respected, but that all children were entitled to be helped to speak Standard English. We could not match this requirement to levels of attainment at primary school because whereas some children speak Standard English at home, others do not. We argued that if children speak dialect at home it is unwise to try to change their speech until at least the age of eight or nine, when they are able to read Standard English and are starting to become familiar with its forms. They can then begin to understand that in speech Standard English gives them an additional form of language of great power socially and in the academic world. In *Cox on Cox* I included a whole chapter on the reasons why children must learn to read and write Standard English. In this book I deal with Standard English again in chapter 5.

Creative writing

We argued that children need to engage regularly in the craft of writing, to use language in structured ways to communicate their own emotions and ideas. Teachers also should write, so that they can serve as role models for children, and share with their pupils their own pieces of work. We believed that all children should write in a variety of forms: fiction, verse, drama, reviews, diaries, autobiography, expository prose.

I am Chair of the Arvon Foundation, which uses three houses in Devon, Yorkshire and near Inverness for five-day courses in the craft of writing, all taught by professional writers. In 1995 we launched a campaign to persuade all training institutions that teachers of English should practise the art of writing, and that all teacher-trainees should attend Arvon-style courses. One of the founders of the Arvon Foundation was Ted Hughes, the Poet Laureate. His book, *Poetry in the Making* (1967), has been very influential in encouraging children and teachers to write. For over thirty years he has been involved in judging the W.H. Smith annual Children's Literary Competition. He wrote recently about this experience in a letter of 7 December 1993 to the Chair of the NEAB examining group. Ted Hughes was critical of a decision to drop Creative Writing from 'A' level:

❥ the verbal creative skills of schoolchildren in the UK are of an astonishing abundance and variety, but this abundance and quality are entirely dependent on the individual teacher.... the proportion of exceedingly high quality writing has risen through the three decades, but especially during the last decade, reflecting a pervasively increasing skill in the teachers and an increasing number of teachers with access to this skill.... all this creative and in many cases richly cultivated ability is – almost without exception – utterly destroyed soon after the pupil leaves school.

This is one reason for the Arvon Foundation. The destruction is partly because so many courses in English for older pupils and in higher education include no creative writing. Unfortunately creative writing was given a bad name in the 1960s when some teachers advocated an 'anything goes' policy, encouraging children to write freely without the discipline of craft. Ted Hughes writes:

❥ the present much-publicised backlash against the general concept of 'creative writing' has been provoked, as we all know, by a certain mode of teaching, introduced through the last three decades by ill-trained and sometimes politically-motivated teachers, who simply stole the term 'creative writing' to dignify their travesty.... As any first-hand experience of the work of good English teachers shows, properly taught 'creative writing' is a rigorous discipline that calls on the activity of the whole mind – incidentally releasing enormous energy for other classroom purposes.

Arvon's aim is to ensure that by the end of the century all teachers of English should find pleasure in their own skills in the craft of writing. This campaign follows on directly from the recommendations of the Cox Report.

Multicultural education

In *Cox on Cox* I explained why texts in English from other cultures should be an essential feature of a national curriculum: '*If we are to live together harmoniously in a multicultural society, we must tolerate each other's way of life, learn to compromise, and even to admire, where appropriate, forms of behaviour and feeling and thought very different from our own.*' (p.154)

The most dynamic English today is often found outside Britain, from writers in Africa, Australia, Canada, India, the West Indies or the United States. In *Cox on Cox* I described (p.74) how Angela Rumbold,

Conservative Minister of State for Education, changed the attainment target for Reading in the 1989 curriculum at the last minute, removing the requirement to read 'works from different cultures'. When challenged in the *TES* on this revision, she replied that the Programmes of Study, which have statutory force, still included the requirement that for all stages in the curriculum reading materials should 'include works written in English from other cultures', and that there was no decision to downgrade the study of literature from other cultures in the English curriculum. When in 1992 the NCC decided to revise the English curriculum it soon became apparent that the lists of set authors would include very few non-British writers, with an occasional name such as Derek Walcott thrown in as a token gesture. I discuss in chapter 10 the need for multicultural texts in a national curriculum.

Changes in teaching English since the 1960s

As I was one of the editors of the Black Papers, which in 1969 started a campaign which placed great emphasis on the importance of basics in education, I am often asked whether over the years my views have changed. I reply that the Cox Report is strong on basics such as spelling, handwriting and the need to write clear, accurate prose, but in some respects my views have indeed changed during the last twenty-five years. These shifts reflect major developments in linguistics, literary theory and the teaching of English which are accepted by most professional teachers both in schools and higher education. A major problem when the NCC decided to revise the English curriculum was that some of its members were ignorant of these developments, and insofar as they did know about them they were often strongly prejudiced against them. Some members of NCC and SEAC were unsympathetic to almost all the research in linguistics of the last thirty years. There are three areas in particular where my own views reflect widespread changes in attitudes to the teaching of English language and literature: new understanding of the rules of language, the use of coursework in assessment, and broader ideas about a canon of authors appropriate for study.

Rules of language

I have already given several examples of how attitudes to language have changed over the last three or four decades. The change is seen in the way teachers of linguistics use the word 'correct'. Let me stress again that children must be helped to write and speak Standard English with clarity and precision, and that they must be corrected when their usage is sloppy or ambiguous. But in the 1950s when I was an undergraduate we took it for granted that the English language should obey Latinate rules, and that the 'correct' forms of language were fixed immutably. All linguists now accept that Standard English keeps changing, and, as I have already shown, that the Standard English I use (aged 66) is not the same as that spoken today by highly educated young graduates. *The Oxford Companion to the English Language* (1992) gives examples of these shifts. The most obvious is that young speakers and writers split their infinitives without being aware that the matter was ever controversial. There are more subtle shifts, particularly in forms of politeness. Words such as 'would' and 'might' are used by my generation to express hesitation or politeness, and such usages are disappearing.

Perhaps most important, our attitudes in the 1990s to gender and race are reflected in shifts in language. Today no sensible MP would use 'he' as a generic pronoun. MPs say 'he or she' so not to annoy their female supporters. Elderly English academics have been booed in the United States when they have used 'boys' to mean all children. I used these examples to illustrate changes in vocabulary when I was interviewed about National Curriculum English by Sir Ron Dearing in the Summer of 1993. He was quite animated in replying that these distinctions may concern teachers but are of no importance in the real world of business. He could not be more wrong. This shift in language marks revolutionary changes in the status of women which many men over the age of 60 find it very difficult to accept.

Similarly, no MP today would call some of their constituents 'half-castes'. They would say 'of mixed race', for 'half-caste' implies contempt. This was not true in the 1930s. No one uses the term 'nigger' today except as a form of abuse. We are more aware today of the dangers of racism.

Many older Conservatives find these changes deeply disturbing, and are upset when they hear that such matters are discussed in school. They fear the breakdown of forms of authority which in previous generations were implied in upper-class pronunciation and language use. In an article in *The Independent Magazine* on 2 November 1990, Stephen Spender said that before 1945 it was taken for granted that children of every kind of social background (particularly from the working class) should ideally speak and write an English which conformed with the standards of the best speech and writing of the educated upper classes.

The purpose of teaching them the traditional classics was that they should meet these standards. There really were no other standards. But in recent years we hear on the BBC new accents, new voices. Today our schools include thousands of children from various ethnic communities. The idea of 'correct English as Received Pronunciation' is no longer valid. And, as I have shown, the vocabulary and grammar of Standard English shifts from generation to generation. The great tradition of Milton, Keats or Jane Austen, Spender says, is growing even further away from the present fluid Anglo-American language. He writes: '*The idea of a future in which there is no single standard but a multiplicity of standards, each with its separate variety of correctness, is indeed terrifying.*'

The 1989 English curriculum encouraged teachers to discuss these issues with their pupils, to consider what 'correct' means, and how language use needs to be appropriate to the social context. We wanted pupils to be introduced to a dynamic rather than a stagnant idea of Standard English, and we believed that if children became fascinated by language in use their own performance in writing would improve.

Coursework

My experiences in 1964 as a teacher in the Department of English at the University of California at Berkeley confronted me with the problems of plagiarism, cheating and bullying of teachers often encouraged by assessment based on coursework. In England at that time coursework was not used for assessment, so all this was new to me. A student told me that if I gave him a grade 'C' for his essay it proved I was a bad teacher. Another seemed to me to have stolen material from a book of literary criticism, but I could not track down his source. In England, teachers say they can easily deduce when a pupil is being helped by parents, but I do not accept this. A clever parent can make minor changes to improve accuracy which may go undetected. And middle-class parents will drive twenty miles to transport their child to a library or museum to collect materials, an advantage not available to children of parents with low incomes.

These are some of the reasons why I do not support the English teachers who advocate 100 per cent coursework for GCSE. But the importance of coursework has increased in recent years because of valuable changes in teaching methods. I am quite happy at GCSE, for example, for assessment to be based on 80 per cent coursework and 20 per cent on traditional exams.

Coursework is the *only* way of assessing dramatic activities and creative writing – both, as I have urged, vital elements in a national curriculum for English. Some people argue that exams should be limited to basics, such as spelling and accurate use of prose. As I said in my Introduction, the danger of this reductive approach is that pressure is put on teachers to concentrate on what is examined, particularly if the results are published in league tables, and to neglect enriching curriculum activities which can only be assessed by coursework.

The canon

In the 1950s university English departments often insisted that authors for study should be chosen exclusively from British writers from Chaucer to T.S. Eliot. T.S. Eliot and Henry James were accepted into the canon because they were naturalised Englishmen. Ezra Pound was unacceptable, in spite of his considerable influence on twentieth-century writing, while in courses on the novel Tolstoy, Dostoyevsky or Flaubert were not allowed into the canon because students would have to read them in translation. In some departments these absurdities existed even into the 1990s. I have already explained why I now advocate that a national curriculum should include texts from other cultures. Central to the Cox curriculum was an idea of balance. We need national unity, for common understanding of Standard English, for common values of justice and equality and freedom of expression so we can live at peace with each other. We need to maintain our cultural heritage, our knowledge of English classics of high quality such as Shakespeare, Wordsworth, Jane Austen, Dickens or the Brontes, whose writings so much influenced the English language. At the same time we need to respect local differences, the need for diversity in our multicultural society, so that we may respect each other's dialect, each other's culture, each other's religion. It is this tension between unity and diversity to which the Cox Report addressed itself.

The balances it proposes are not easy to achieve. We were attacked by the Right Wing who wanted stability and unity based on the hegemony imposed by the upper and middle classes in the 1930s and before. We were attacked by the Left Wing because we advocated that all children should study Shakespeare and the literature of the past, our English inheritance, and that they should speak and write Standard English. I feel particularly angry that this balance was set aside when the English curriculum was redrafted by NCC in 1993.

LINC: Language in the National Curriculum

After the publication in 1989 of the Cox Report a major project was launched to help teachers to understand the model of language recommended in the Kingman Report of 1988, the model on which the Cox proposals were based. This was the Language in the National Curriculum (LINC) project under the direction of Professor Ronald Carter at Nottingham University. Professor Carter works in a department of English studies, and is at present head of one of the most highly-ranked teaching and research departments in the country (according to the Government's own measures). This project proved invaluable in helping teachers to devise programmes of study for knowledge about language. This work was commissioned by Kenneth Baker as Secretary of State for Education, and from 1989 to 1992 £21 million was invested in the LINC project, mainly on teacher training. From schools all over the country, teachers designated by their heads as language coordinators for the whole school spent occasional days at training sessions. Teachers from almost every primary and secondary school in England and Wales were trained using materials developed by a team of 25 coordinators and trialled in every local education authority in the country. In the last year of the project there were nearly 400 training courses involving 10,000 teachers nationally.

In 1991 Professor Carter and his team prepared 500 pages of materials designed to help teachers to improve their pupils' knowledge about language. In June 1991, by which time Kenneth Clarke was Secretary of State for Education, the Government decided to suppress these materials, and even tried to prevent Professor Carter from publishing them commercially. Professor Carter complained bitterly that it was an abrogation of freedom of speech to refuse to waive Crown copyright on the materials: commercial publication would allow the issues to be debated openly.

In *The Oxford Companion to the English Language* (1992) Christopher Brumfit of Southampton University writes about LINC: '*In the opinion of many observers, the long-standing conflict between the views of Conservative politicians on the role of language and those of linguists and educationists reached a new stage with an act of direct official censorship.*' (p.269) Why did Ministers refuse to publish the LINC materials? The decision was explained in the *TES* of 28 June 1991 by Tim Eggar, Minister of State for Education, who said the materials were '*not designed, nor are they suitable,*

for classoom use as teaching materials.' Professor Carter replied that Mr
Eggar was confusing training materials and classroom materials. The
brief for the project was to produce in-service training materials, suitable
for staff development through the 1990s. It was never Mr Baker's
intention that classroom materials should be produced. Mr Eggar's
comments that the materials might get into the wrong hands, be used
out of context, or be misunderstood in schools was deeply patronising to
teachers.

Mr Eggar's real objections were that the materials included too many
examples of children's work which were poor in quality, too many drawn
from the media which dealt with 'controversial matters in a biased way',
and too much prominence was given to exceptions rather than the
norm, to dialects rather than Standard English, for example. The section
on accents, dialects and Standard English, Mr Eggar complained, was
mostly concerned with non-standard English; it represented a *'distraction
from the main task of teaching children to write, spell and punctuate correctly.*
Professor Carter replied that the LINC materials did include a section on
grammar, and that the project was intended to help teachers by
disseminating the Kingman model of the English language, rather than
to give specific advice on classroom teaching of writing, spelling and
punctuation.

The LINC materials adopted a balanced and moderate position
towards controversial issues such as the teaching of grammar and the
place of Standard English and dialects in the curriculum. The LINC
materials included a more detailed description of the grammar of
English than in any mother-tongue English curriculum materials
anywhere in the world. The LINC grammar section begins:

❛ Language is used to make, exchange, convey and record meanings
and information. It is able to do these jobs because it works according
to systems that are understood by the people who 'speak the same
language'. Of these systems, grammar is the major one.

The public comments of Kenneth Clarke and Tim Eggar showed that
they know little about such definitions, and had simply absorbed the old-
fashioned traditionalist view that more exercises in grammar would raise
standards in literacy.

The newspapers dealt with this controversy with their usual
confusions and prejudices. The leader in the London *Evening Standard* of
26 June 1991 strongly supported Mr Eggar's decision not to publish the
LINC materials. Professor Carter and his team were called 'barmy' and
'politically-biased'. The leader began:

❝ Mr Tim Eggar, an Education Minister, refuses to waste £120,000 on the publication of a report by educational theorists which recommends, among other things, that dialects should have equal status with the Queen's English in Britain's schools.... it is as though the 'experts' were determined to destroy the concept of correctness in language and literature in the belief that teaching children Standard English and grammar was an oppression of the working class, and one that ran counter to multiculturalism, anti-racism and anti-sexism.

This kind of abuse from irresponsible journalists was based on a complete misrepresentation of the LINC position. Yet most politicians receive their information about English teaching from sources such as the *Evening Standard*. It was very difficult for Professor Carter to combat such wilful perversion of the LINC materials.

There were one or two exceptions to this chorus of disapproval. On 11 July 1991, Colin Hughes wrote an excellent article in the *Independent*, but from this time onwards decisions by Ministers were more influenced by the need to please the popular media than by rational argument in quality newspapers. Hughes explained that English in the 1989 National Curriculum required that all pupils should develop the ability to think and talk about how language works, including an explicit understanding of the different terms of grammar, which should be acquired during their secondary school years: '*The centrality of grammar in other words was to be restored.*' But the problem, Hughes continued, was that the National Curriculum did not require a return to formal grammar teaching. Instead, children should learn about how language works in the context of all their reading and writing: '*Few teachers seriously doubt that this is the most effective way of raising the quality of children's work*'. Hughes commented:

❝ The critical problem with the 'new grammar' is not that it is 'wacky' or 'trendy', or even that it is complacent about standards; it is that the methods are extremely demanding of the teacher, requiring extensive knowledge of language. Moreover, they require that *all* teachers, not just English teachers, become conscious of the way children are using language. In truth, probably only a minority of teachers feel confident about delivering the National Curriculum's language learning targets; many, it must be reasonably suspected, may not have entirely understood them.... It is the combination of scepticism and ignorance among teachers, leading to insecurity and resistance to the notion of teaching grammar, that has to be addressed. That is exactly what the 'Language in the National Curriculum' project set out to do.

The contrast between the wild rhetoric of the *Evening Standard* and the clear arguments of the *Independent* sets the context in which battles over education policy take place.

The LINC authors argued that a better understanding of language can sharpen teachers' appreciation of children's achievement with language and help them to understand the nature of difficulties or partial success. It can guide them in their interventions in children's learning, in which delicate judgments about what to make explicit and what to leave implicit in children's knowledge are so important. A worked-out theory of language in learning equips teachers to discuss with other adults, both fellow professionals and lay people, pupils' achievements and needs in language, and to explain policies to them.

The LINC programme was based on four principles, all very much in tune with recommendations in the 1989 English curriculum:

♦ Extending pupils' knowledge about language should start from what children can do: from their positive achievement in language and from the remarkable resources of implicit knowledge about language which all children possess.

♦ The experience of using language is prior to conscious reflection on or analysis of language. Reflection and analysis can and do influence use, however, as long as they offer users enabling insights into their own or other people's efforts to make meaning in language. Terminology, which is a servant of reflection and analysis, should be employed when a teacher thinks it will help pupils to gain these insights.

♦ Language should be studied in its own right as a rich and fascinating example of human behaviour. It should be explored in real, purposeful situations, not analysed out of context.

♦ An understanding of attitudes to language, of its uses and misuses, can enable pupils to see through language to the underlying ways in which values and beliefs are communicated in it.

My summary of the LINC approach shows that the project offered an invaluable, intelligent survey for teachers preparing to introduce their pupils to knowledge about language. The size of the LINC project shows how much was done between 1989 and 1992 to ensure that language and grammar were taught efficiently. The argument put about by some politicians and journalists that the early years of English in the National Curriculum were a disaster, only rectified by the slimming-down proposals of Sir Ron Dearing, is nonsense. If the 1989 English curriculum had been left unrevised, carefully evaluated by research in the classroom and improved gradually by non-statutory advice, and if the LINC project had continued to be supported by Ministers, there is no doubt standards in schools would be much higher today. From 1991 onwards the morale of teachers of English was undermined by absurd interferences by politicians based on arrogance, ignorance and prejudice.

The history of LINC-related developments since 1992 illustrates the folly of the Government's attempt to censor this work. The training pack, *The LINC Materials for Professional Development*, was printed with the support of local education authorities in a desk-top published version and distributed for use in in-service training sessions. LEAs were initially responsible for distribution but the materials are now obtainable from the Department of English Studies at Nottingham University. The materials are accompanied by five 25-minute BBC TV programmes and five 20-minute BBC radio programmes, available on tape. Over 30,000 copies have been ordered to date and orders continue to flourish. (Nottingham simply covers its costs.) Ironically, it was planned that HMSO should print only 18,000. In addition to extensive use in Britain, the materials are being widely used in Australia, New Zealand, nine States in the USA, Canada, Singapore, Hong Kong and across Europe (in many cases for English as a Foreign Language as well as English Mother Tongue teacher-training). There is universal praise for the materials and for the way they attempt to mediate the Cox Report's vision concerning knowledge about language. There is universal bafflement that materials which are so balanced and moderate could have been refused publication and are only available in this Samizdat form.

Two LINC-related publications published before the end of the project have been considerable successes, both published by Hodder and Stoughton: *Knowledge About Language and the Curriculum: The LINC Reader* (edited by Ronald Carter), a collection of more theoretical papers, and *Looking into Language* (edited by Richard Bain *et al*), a collection of practical classroom-focused papers. The BBC has continued to broadcast the LINC TV programmes according to demand from teachers and to make programmes devoted to grammar (eg *Get the Grammar*, 1994) with ex-LINC coordinators as main writers and presenters. At the same time 'A' level English Language, especially the Manchester-based NEAB curriculum, continues to grow, and is taught by LINC-trained teachers. All this demonstrates how since 1991 important curriculum development has been forced to proceed in separation from the government-sponsored NCC, SEAC and SCAA.

Kenneth Clarke sacks the Professionals

An interview for NCC

Control of the National Curriculum can lead to control of the way children think. A national curriculum in English influences attitudes to class and race, as I demonstrated in my first chapter. The LINC materials encouraged pupils to see through language to the underlying ways in which values and beliefs are communicated. Children need to emerge from school with a highly developed ability to understand how all forms of language are being used and manipulated; many teachers suspected that some Conservatives wanted to ban the LINC materials because they instinctively opposed classroom activities which helped children to analyse the underlying assumptions of political rhetoric.

July 1991 proved a bad month for British democracy. I played a small but symbolic part in the events which enabled a small right-wing pressure group to take over the National Curriculum, though at the time I did not appreciate the significance of what was happening. On Tuesday 9 July I officiated as Pro-Vice-Chancellor at a degree ceremony at the University of Manchester. These formal occasions are always joyous, rites of passage when parents and their offspring celebrate the successful conclusion of their degree courses. The degrees we confer are accepted internationally because they are validated by independent academics, professional men and women who are experts in their subjects.

After the ceremony I returned to the English departmental office where my secretary, Shelagh, presented me with an intriguing message.

Michael Fallon, Parliamentary Under-Secretary of State for Education, wanted me to contact his office urgently. I rang back, and was told by one of his staff that he wished me to travel to London to see him as soon as possible. I asked what he wanted, but I was informed that the matter was confidential, and that my question could not be answered on the phone. As I was busy with degree ceremonies, the first day we could find when we were both free was Thursday 18 July.

When the letter confirming this arrangement arrived it said that the meeting was to discuss 'an appointment to the Public Service'. What did this mean? I was further amazed when a day later I received a fax asking me to submit a curriculum vitae. At 62 years of age and very happy at Manchester University, it was many years since I had kept my c.v. up-to-date. I rang Mr Fallon's office, pointed out that civil servants are forced to retire at 60, and asked again what was this all about. I was told that the work would not take up more than 30 days a year, but that the office could not be more specific.

As I travelled down by train (I received no expenses), I was a little excited and apprehensive about the size of the job I was to be offered. Duncan Graham had just been sacked as Chairman and Chief Executive of the National Curriculum Council, so what kind of reorganisation was taking place? The receptionist at Elizabeth House deflated me by telling me that I was among several people being considered just for membership of the NCC, and this was confirmed by Mr Fallon when he interviewed me. The interview, carried out by Mr Fallon and a Civil Servant, lasted about half an hour, and was quite fierce as we discussed my views of the National Curriculum, and specifically the English Programmes of Study. I was told that they would report to Kenneth Clarke, the Secretary of State for Education, and that he would make the decisions.

When a week later I departed with my wife for a summer holiday, I had heard nothing from Mr Fallon. When I returned on 14 August some appointments to NCC had been announced but for me there were no messages. I thought perhaps he was away on holiday, and so I took no action until early September. I then rang his office, pointing out that I had not even received the courtesy of a thank-you letter. I was told that the interview had not been for membership of the NCC, but was normal practice when Ministers wanted a general chat with people who might be later considered for a public appointment. I replied that this explanation was untrue, that Mr Fallon had said specifically that I was being considered for membership of the NCC, and that not even to thank me for making a special journey to London was downright rude. I demanded an apology.

A week later a letter arrived from Mr Fallon, saying he was sorry if there had been any misunderstanding of the basis for our discussions on Thursday, 18 July, and indeed my qualifications were not thought appropriate for the kind of balance Kenneth Clarke wanted at that time for the NCC. Presumably I was interviewed because my work on the Black Papers of 1969 to 1977 had led someone to think that I would sympathise with the dogmatists of the right. During my interview with Michael Fallon I argued that it was unfortunate that the Government had refused to allow the LINC materials on the teaching of English language to be published. This interference, I argued, would damage the new interest in language, including grammar, which the 1989 document had generated. I also argued that the morale of the teachers was alarmingly low, and that a top priority must be encouragement and support for the profession.

On the Friday after the interview the *TES* published a review of my book *Cox on Cox: An English Curriculum for the 1990s*, by Peter Hollindale of York University. He quoted some lines from the first chapter of my book: '*Conservative politicians were over-confident that they knew the right policies, and to a large extent were contemptuous towards the professional teacher.*' Hollindale said that I was an 'expert', and that the Government was determined on 'rubbishing the experts'. He wrote that *Cox on Cox* '*gives an hilarious account of the muddle and misinformation which led Kenneth Baker and his colleagues, under the false impression that they were choosing a bunch of safe backwoodsmen who would advocate traditional grammar, to appoint by mistake a highly intelligent and enlightened committee fully capable of producing a worthy English curriculum.*' It seems possible that before Kenneth Clarke rejected me for the NCC, one of his advisers drew his attention to this review. At my degree ceremonies we celebrated degree courses and qualifications validated by experts. Neither I nor presumably Peter Hollindale realised how in July 1991 we were seeing the start of a great battle for control of the National Curriculum, a battle which continues to the present day, and which began with the removal of power from the professionals.

Takeover at NCC and SEAC

This account of my interview illustrates the high-handed and secretive way in which after 1991 the Conservatives were packing quangos with their own supporters. The process begun by Kenneth Clarke in 1991 was continued by John Patten when after the General Election in 1992 he became Secretary of State for Education. Clarke replaced Graham as Chair of NCC with David Pascall, a BP oil executive who had previously been a member of Mrs Thatcher's Downing Street Policy Unit. Philip Halsey at SEAC was replaced by Lord Brian Griffiths. Duncan Graham had previously worked as Chief Executive of Humberside County Council and County Education Officer in Suffolk; Philip Halsey was a former Civil Servant of impeccable neutrality. In contrast, Lord Griffiths had previously been heavily involved in politics as head of the Downing Street Policy Unit; he was also chair of the right-wing Centre for Policy Studies. A lay preacher, he was determined with missionary zeal to take education out of the hands of the professionals and to restore what he considered to be the successful traditional practices of the 1950s. Two of his sub-chairmen, Dr John Marks, who chaired the Mathematics Committee, and Dr John Marenbon, who chaired the English Committee, were also closely identified with the Centre for Policy Studies. John Marks was secretary of its education study group. John Marenbon, as noted in my first chapter, was married to Sheila Lawlor, its deputy director. John Patten placed John Marks on NCC in July 1992, where he was to prove very influential.

David Pascall was first appointed to NCC in 1990 by John McGregor, then the Secretary of State for Education, on the advice of his long-time golfing friend Bob Horton, Chairman of BP. Pascall was later happy to recount how his name had come up on the eighteenth green and this had changed his life, because until then he had no interest in or knowledge of the National Curriculum.

The young, forceful David Pascall disliked the NCC under Duncan Graham. There were too many 'experts' and officials at the table and too many papers to be mastered. When Kenneth Clarke succeeded McGregor, Pascall sought an early audience and told him that only a streamlined Council of the like-minded could deliver the 'plain man's' curriculum. Clarke agreed. His decision to fire Duncan Graham was not too unpopular with teachers because Graham had been associated with the deluge of documents and directives which had alarmed schools in the previous two years. Pascall became part-time Chairman, with Chris Woodhead as Chief Executive. Pascall, a graduate of a tough MBA school, would guarantee to deliver the goods; Woodhead would know how to fashion the goods to be delivered.

Other influential members of NCC left the Council. Paul Black, Professor of Science Education at King's College, London, ended his term of office. Black had steered through the Science Orders, which were fiercely opposed as too complex and demanding. The subsequent history of those Science Orders as they were rewritten and hacked with scissors and paste four times made for four years of unnecessary upheaval and expense in schools. Curiously, for a government opposed to waste, there was never any shortage of money for the NCC, as it owned two buildings in York, while building a third by the river (over the reputed palace of Emperor Septimius Severus) on a site which regularly floods. Clarke cleared out seven members in all, and largely gave Pascall a free hand in selecting the replacements. Pascall chose some old friends from his Policy Unit days like Graham Mackenzie, Chief Executive of Midland Engineers, Brian Hutchinson of BAT, Professor David Regan of Nottingham University who was a member of 'The Educational Research Trust', a right-wing evangelical Christian group (its Director was Dr John Marks and advisers included Lord Brian Griffiths), and Pascall's own daughter's headmistress, Mrs Joan Clanchy of the North London Collegiate School. These joined the rump of the old Council, 'safe' figures like John McIntosh, Mrs Thatcher's favourite headmaster, and Jennifer Wisker, Education Officer for Somerset.

The new Council, which met in September in an hotel in Rutland to do some 'bonding' exercises in the style of management practice, was to be quite different from the old one. No officials (except Chris Woodhead) were to be at the table; they were to sit at the back of the room and not contribute to the debate. Meetings were to start with a dinner without any official present and no minutes. The Quango was in charge.

The first item was revision mark one of the Science Orders, which it is safe to say no one on the Council properly understood. Clarke wanted them easy to test; therefore they had to be simplified. They were hacked about, but the difficulties that were then pushed into the top attainment levels were not resolved and the troubles were certain to return.

The next items were the introduction of the Music and Art Orders due to be published in December 1991. The Working Group in Music had been headed by Sir John Manduell, Head of the Royal Northern College of Music, a highly respected figure with traditionalist views. They were not traditional enough for the new tough Council, which knew better than he did. John McIntosh, who was pleased to claim to be something of an amateur organist, was assigned to toughen the Order up and generally ensure that the emphasis on the West European cultural tradition was recognisable to the lay man. The same was done to Art. The two versions of the Music curriculum were given to the Council members only 48 hours before the meeting. Many of the members, especially from the rump that had not been purged in July, were uneasy. They were unhappy at the emphasis away from 'making music' to 'learning about music'. The debate was interrupted by two fire alarms. Finally, by a majority of one, the McIntosh version won, but the minority was assured that there would be modifications to take account of their views. There were none. The Orders were published in January to the delight of such papers as the *Daily Mail*, not noted for a deep interest in cultural matters, but which saw at once that this was bashing trendy music teachers and was a blow for Beethoven over reggae. A formidable number of distinguished musicians, led by Simon Rattle, protested loudly, but to no avail. Under the new regime, John McIntosh knew more about music than Simon Rattle.

The rows over Music and Art polarised the members of the Council. The minority which had opposed the radical changes to the Music Working Group's Orders were now the official opposition. The atmosphere was charged at the January 1992 meeting when a letter from Kenneth Clarke invited NCC to consider the English Orders again (and, by implication, to do to them what had been done to Music and Art). Pascall showed all his charm and management skills in calming the unrest. The matter should be deferred. Besides an election was looming and there was no point in getting into such a row in the spring of 1992. It was a time to placate teachers, indeed to give them their full pay award. The Council got on with trying to make sense of the new initiatives over Key Stage 4 testing. English waited until after the Election. Passing reference was made to the study of the working of the English Orders being undertaken by Professor Raban of Warwick University, but the Council at its 'management training' weekend had already agreed to give low priority to academic research.

What is so disturbing about these events is the ease with which such a small group of like-minded campaigners were able to take over the National Curriculum, with little public knowledge of what was happening. Kenneth Clarke was determined to strengthen Whitehall's control of the curriculum and its assessment. One of Lord Griffiths's first decisions at SEAC, akin to that by Pascall at NCC, was to make it clear to the Department of Education and Science and HMI assessors that their presence was no longer required at meetings. All these right-wingers were sincere, honest and passionately committed to their educational beliefs. They were willing to work hard; the results of their labours were to cause major disruption in our schools for several years.

There were still some non-conformist members of NCC and SEAC - such as Joan Clanchy, who resigned from NCC in February 1993, and

Peter Harding, head of English at Carre's Grammar School, Sleaford, Lincolnshire, who while still a member of its English Committee wrote a vigorous attack on SEAC in the *TES* on 15 January 1993 - but, as they both confirmed, the right-wing traditionalists were in the majority. Early decisions were made to reduce the coursework component in GCSE to around 20–30 per cent, to give all fourteen-year-olds tests on Shakespeare and grammar, to place more emphasis on the British Empire and on facts and dates in History, and to order the Northern Examining Board to take references to *Coronation Street* and *Neighbours* out of its syllabus.

Political control of the curriculum

How was it possible for Kenneth Clarke to hand over control of NCC and SEAC so easily to a small, extreme right-wing group? Unfortunately Kenneth Baker failed to provide proper safeguards when he set up the National Curriculum in the Education Reform Act of 1988. In his autobiography, *The View from No.11*, (1992) Nigel Lawson says of Kenneth Baker that '*not even his greatest friends would describe him as either a profound political thinker or a man with a mastery of detail. His instinctive answer to any problem is to throw glossy PR and large quantities of money at it, and his favoured brand of politics is the instant response to the cry of the moment*' (p.606).

In his *A Lesson for Us All: The Making of the National Curriculum* (1992), Duncan Graham tells how in 1988 he was called down to London by Kenneth Baker to be offered the job of Chairman and Chief Executive of the National Curriculum Council. The meeting, he says, was 'gloriously unspecific': '*He offered me a concept of what the job was even if the details were decidedly vague*' (p.9). Graham was an energetic administrator determined to make the curriculum work, and that meant careful attention to detail. As soon as he began to take action, he discovered that Baker's woolliness continually left him (Graham) in an exposed position, unsure of his powers and responsibilities.

The situation had reached crisis level as early as the spring of 1989, when NCC addressed the problem of what came to be known as the whole curriculum, a phrase Graham soon realised to be politically unacceptable. Teachers knew that in addition to the ten obligatory subjects the curriculum must include more general themes. NCC listed five: citizenship, environment, economic and industrial understanding, careers and health. It proposed to publish five booklets, and immediately was opposed by Kenneth Baker, who presumably realised he might be committing himself to left-wing ideology. He clearly had given no thought to the status of these themes in a national curriculum. Graham won this battle, and he tells us that the pamphlets were soon in use in most schools, but already it was apparent that the NCC's independence would be perpetually under threat from Graham's political masters.

The main, overriding problem was that there were no clear guidelines about who should take final control over the curriculum. When I was appointed Chair of the English Working Group, I assumed – perhaps naively – that my duty was to produce a curriculum which reflected the best of professional advice and classroom practice. Saunders Watson, who chaired the History Working Group, took a similar stance, and as a result Mrs Thatcher decided he had gone native, and let the country down. She was determined, like Lord Griffiths and Dr Marks, that the History curriculum should place great emphasis on the learning of historical facts; in contrast, the History Working Group rejected parrot learning, and said that names, dates and places provide only the starting-points for understanding. As with the English proposals, the extreme right-wing feared interpretation and analysis, and wanted obedient pupils to learn facts and obey authority. In an article in the *Daily Telegraph* (6 May 1993) Bethan Marshall compared the ideas of this group to those of Mr Gradgrind in Dickens's *Hard Times*. The comparison was also used by Paul Foot in a delicious satire of the Centre for Policy Studies group in *Private Eye* (21 May 1993).

Graham says that Baker told him after his appointment that ministers had insisted on a National Curriculum Council because they realised they would need totally independent professional advice over and beyond the kind they would get from civil servants. Teachers would also need a source of independent educational advice, and it would be better if schools were given that advice by people they saw as professionally credible. Graham writes: '*Both Baker and Rumbold believed there were dangers in the National Curriculum if it passed into the hands of an unscrupulous minister and that the existence of NCC with a strong professional view would be a bulwark*' (p.113).

These dangers became reality when Kenneth Clarke was appointed Secretary of State. He interfered decisively in the row over the History curriculum, deciding on his own initiative that modern history, studied by children aged 14 – 16, should run from the turn of the century to a time twenty years before the present. He established that the Secretary of State was in charge of the curriculum, and could manipulate it to serve political ends.

As I have shown, from 1991 onwards NCC and SEAC were packed with members of the right-wing establishment. Peter Dines, Secretary of NCC until he retired in August 1991, was quoted in the *Independent on Sunday* (2 August 1992) saying that these appointments to NCC were 'very close to being against the law'. To fulfil its statutory functions it must be independent. Also in the summer of 1992, Eric Bolton, who had just retired as the senior Chief Inspector of Schools and then been elected Professor of Teacher Education at London University's Institute of Education, told a conference of local education authorities that the Government was listening only to fashionable voices on the right, and that the influence of right-wing think tanks on education appeared stronger under Mr Major than under Mrs Thatcher: '*There is no crime in listening to your political friends,*' Professor Bolton said, '*but a wise government listens more widely than that, and especially to those with no political axe to grind. It is not auspicious that the former channels of advice about education to the Government appear either to be being muzzled (HMI), or packed with people likely to say whatever the Government wants to hear (the NCC and SEAC)*' (2 August 1992, in the *Independent on Sunday*). Baroness Blatch, Education Minister of State in 1992, tried to rebut Professor Bolton's accusations, but repeated the Centre for Policy Studies' rhetoric about the educational professionals who had given us education without structure, and education without grammar and spelling.

In 1993 NCC and SEAC were brought together as the School Curriculum and Assessment Authority (SCAA). When its members were announced, well-known right-wingers such as Dr Marks and Professor Philip O'Hear were members.

All political parties ought to recognise that SCAA should be independent and seen to be independent. Members should be appointed not by the Minister, but by independent institutions (head teachers' associations, for example, together with a representative of the Confederation of British Industry and another from the Trade Union Congress). The need to wrest control of the curriculum from political interference and to return it to an independent body is vital for our children's future.

Rhetoric of the Right

The kind of rhetoric common to this small group of ultra-Conservatives was seen in a speech given by Dr Marks at the Institute of Economic

Affairs in November 1992, entitled 'The National Curriculum and Primary School Method' at a conference on 'Education and Choice in Britain and America' attended by delegates from both Britain and America. In his speech Marks combined two elements characteristic of rhetoric from Centre for Policy Studies' members: fantasies about what was really happening in British classrooms, and misunderstandings of recent developments in linguistics, media studies and the teaching of English. Common *fantasies* were as follows:

◆ Pervasive left-wing influence was said by Marks to be responsible for a major decline in educational standards, particularly in reading. His lecture mixed up references to left-wing theorists such as Professor Terry Eagleton with anecdotes about low standards in schools.

◆ Left-wing teachers are ruining standards in reading by refusing to use phonic methods, and by promoting the utopian 'real books' method of teaching reading, in which children are supposed to learn naturally without instruction in phonics because of their pleasure in 'real books'. I deal with this fantasy in detail later in this chapter, and also in chapter 3 when I discuss the Warwick research, which shows that most teachers were using phonic methods.

◆ Marks argued that '*the effective reform of primary education will not be achieved without considerable opposition from the educational establishment – both from those with misguided concepts of professionalism and professional practice and from those who want to use education for their own political purposes.*' He illustrated what is happening in classrooms with the story of an enthusiastic young primary school teacher who resigned after being told that '*teaching spelling is against the ethos of the school*'. Such daft ideas about spelling were by no means unusual before the William Tyndale School scandal of 1976, but in the 1990s it would be difficult to find a primary school teacher who believed spelling was not important. This kind of rhetoric, often repeated by politicians such as Kenneth Clarke and in tabloid newspapers, greatly harmed teacher morale. As all teachers knew, the 1989 English National Curriculum made Spelling an essential attainment target, and any state school which treated spelling as 'against the ethos of the school' was breaking the law.

◆ Teachers of English are intent on getting rid of the teaching of Shakespeare and the classics, on denying children 'access to the riches of English literature and our cultural heritage'.This belief, to some extent repeated in speeches by Prince Charles, bears little relation to what was going on in classrooms.

◆ Teachers of English neglect to give their pupils 'a proper understanding of the English language'. In fact, as I have shown, teachers welcomed the recommendations in the 1989 National Curriculum for programmes on knowledge about language.

◆ Marks said, with some degree of truth, that '*the teaching of English has become the main ideological battleground in Britain for those who want to politicise education in a left-wing direction.*' He continued: '*English is to the school curriculum today what sociology was in the universities and polytechnics in the attempted Marxist takeover of higher education in the 1960s. The key difference is that sociology was taken by relatively few students but English is compulsory for all our children.*' This fantasy also bears little relation to what was going on in schools. From the 1980s onwards moderate views prevailed – among teachers, HMIs, advisers and the National Association of Teachers of English. Marxists in the school staff room were few, and Marks had been carried away by speeches by a few militant left-wingers mainly based in London. Above all, the belief that the Cox curriculum needed to be rewritten to eradicate left-wing influence was absurd.

These *fantasies* were mixed up with numerous *misunderstandings*:

◆ For Marks 'a proper understanding of the English language' means old-fashioned grammar lessons. He fails to understand the ideas about language incorporated in the Kingman Report and the Cox curriculum. Many followers of the Centre for Policy Studies, such as Professor Arthur Pollard, who in 1992 became a member of the SEAC English Committee, reject almost all the findings of modern linguists as anathema.

◆ In the Cox Report we described a number of 'views' of the purpose of teaching English. Two of these deal with culture, and they are often quoted:

(a) a 'cultural heritage' view emphasises the responsibility of schools to lead children to an appreciation of those works of literature that have been widely regarded as amongst the finest in the language.

(b) a 'cultural analysis' view emphasises the role of English in helping children towards a critical understanding of the world and cultural environment in which they live. Children should know about the processes by which meanings are conveyed, and about the ways in which print and other media carry values (ch.2). This belief that an English curriculum should incorporate cultural analysis goes back at least as far as F.R. Leavis and Denys Thompson, in the 1930s,

who thought children should be helped to understand the rhetoric of advertisements. In his speech Marks repeated words similar to those used by the Prime Minister on several occasions: 'Many people were surprised that '*Allo, 'Allo* and other television soaps should be seriously proposed as part of a GCSE English Literature course.' Like many right-wing politicians Marks seemed unaware of the arguments in favour of media studies (see chapters 9 and 10). Good teachers often examine how Dickens's use of the serial form, for example, is continued by modern soaps. Above all, media studies help pupils to analyse the forms of culture and language most dominant among their peer group.

◆ Marks quoted educationalists saying that 'the traditional teaching of Shakespeare is "arse-achingly boring" '. He used this to illustrate that English teachers do not wish to teach Shakespeare. He failed to mention that for most pupils the traditional teaching of Shakespeare, which he and his group tried to reintroduce in 1993, *was* boring, and often put pupils off Shakespeare for life. In recent years good teachers have helped pupils to enjoy Shakespeare by involving them in role play and dramatic performance. This successful work was seriously harmed by SEAC's proposals for old-fashioned testing at Key Stage 3.

◆ I agree with Marks's attacks on the relativism of some literary theorists who reject the notion of quality implied in the very concept of 'literature' as a form superior to other kinds of text. I too oppose those academics who refuse to accept that there is a canon of great books, and that all children are entitled to be helped to enjoy such works. But our ideas of the canon constantly change, and a list of great books should never be inscribed in a parliamentary Order, and so written in stone. I believe that we study great books because of their aesthetic value (and that leads to disagreements about what we mean by 'aesthetics'), but we may well find the values of such works distasteful. This distinction should be something pupils are encouraged to discuss. All this does not mean that we should force great books on children at too early an age. In the *London Review of Books* (22 December 1994), in a review of Harold Bloom's defence of a canon of great works, *The Western Canon*, Frank Kermode wrote: '*The preservation of a canon against neglect, but also against its more active enemies, is vital to our better health. It cannot be done by forcing* Julius Caesar *or* A Midsummer Night's Dream *on fifteen-year-olds; many will despise them....*' Marks seemed unaware of these debates, and of the urgent need to ensure that we do not succumb to bardolatry when we study Shakespeare. 'Cultural analysis' of the values implied in his plays is an essential part of good English teaching.

I deal in chapter 6 with John Marenbon's extraordinary anthology for Key Stage 3, and his apparent ignorance, as with Marks, of how choices of literary texts reflect a value system.

Standards

Members of this Conservative group all believed that standards in state schools were in decline, and that National Curriculum English had served to promote the cause of the progressives who had dominated education in the 1960s. The popularity of the Cox curriculum in the schools was not seen by them as a virtue, but a sign that the National Curriculum had only served to confirm the prejudices of fashionable progressive teachers. Neither David Pascall nor Lord Brian Griffiths knew much about the complex issues involved in the teaching of grammar, reading or Standard English, because they had never taught English in the classroom.

This belief that standards were in decline was fuelled by the great controversy over the teaching of reading which became headline news in July 1990. In that month psychologists from nine local authorities in the South and Midlands published statistics showing large falls in young children's reading standards. In the tabloid newspapers these statistics were used for emotional attacks on the teaching profession. The spokesperson for the psychologists was Martin Turner, who in subsequent years made major contributions to the work of the Conservatives who took over the National Curriculum. Turner published his evidence in August in a pamphlet called *Sponsored Reading Failure* (IEA Education Unit, Warlingham Park School, Chesham Common, Warlingham, Surrey, 1990), which also attracted much publicity. Turner argued that the supposed decline in reading standards was due to the fashion for the 'real books' approach to the teaching of reading. This approach, often associated with the writings of Frank Smith, when it is used in an extreme way rejects all structured teaching through practice in phonics and relies on encouraging children to read by providing them with books they will enjoy. Turner said that in the mid-1980s 'hot gospellers' promoted their story-book methods *'producing bigots, converts, heretics and martyrs all over the humdrum classrooms of the nation'*.

The statistics Turner provided did not stand up to careful scrutiny. He produced no evidence except hearsay about the methods used in the schools whose statistics he published. His descriptions of what went on in a typical school were wildly inaccurate, and this is proved conclusively by the Warwick research (see chapter 3) which says: '*In learning to read, phonics activities were the ones which pupils experienced most often and for the longest time*' (p. 117). There was no evidence that at this time a decline in reading standards was due to the adoption by teachers of the 'real books' method. Reading standards were certainly too low, but there were many reasons: social conditions, television, lack of permanent staff in some schools. The issue is always complex, and there are no easy solutions.

The Turner statistics had an immense influence on popular views of standards in schools, and Turner's pamphlet damaged the reputation of the teaching profession. In his pamphlet he accused teachers of being 'preoccupied with the epic of promotion', and of sacrificing children's need to their own career ambitions. Many of the new members of NCC and SEAC accepted Turner's writings as true, and he himself became a member of the English Committee of SEAC. Not surprisingly, from 1991 onwards NCC did not rush to publish the Warwick findings which proved that Turner's allegations about the teaching profession were false. In his pamphlet he attacked National Curriculum English, never mentioning that its requirements for the teaching of reading included a *mix* of methods, including phonics.

Turner's writings had considerable influence because politicians read about them in the press, and few had actually read his pamphlet *Sponsored Reading Failure*. His prose indulges in extraordinary rhetoric which for any sensible reader must immediately cast doubt on all his judgments. The following sentence is not untypical. He is arguing that children should not be used for sociological experiments: '*Children in state schools are not guinea pigs for an irrelevant sociological agenda of race, sex, class, ever-multiplying affronts to the spiritual unity of mankind, the small change of contemporary intellectual ferment (if ferment is not putting it too strongly) in this age of unprecedented intellectual poverty.*'

Do we really live in an age of intellectual poverty? This is the kind of nostalgia for a supposed golden age which runs through so much writing of the Conservatives who took over the National Curriculum in 1991. They see educational issues as a simple battle against progressives, and do not take kindly to complexities. This was shown when the *Guardian* (20 April 1993) printed an article by Martin Turner attacking me as a disciple of Frank Smith and the 'anarchist' Gramsci. Such absurd accusations were repeated again and again by this right-wing group. I shall talk about nostalgia again when in chapter 6 I deal with the Key Stage 3 anthology produced by Dr John Marenbon in 1993.

I have been involved in arguments about standards since I helped to edit the Black Papers in 1969. At that time it was argued that standards had improved since the end of the war in 1945 because of the introduction of progressive teaching methods. I argued that the improvement since 1945 stemmed more from the fact that standards at that time were low, because of the effects of air-raids and the departure of so many teachers to fight in the war. There was no evidence that standards had improved since the 1930s. I repeated many times that the best schools combined the best of traditional and progressive methods of education. I soon learnt that this debate produces stock reactions from the press, which always will print lurid stories about low standards.

Indeed, these have been appearing regularly for at least the last 100 years. In 1912 the English Association reported that '*it is a plain fact that the average boy or girl on leaving school is unable to write English with clearness and fluency or with any degree of grammatical accuracy... It is a common experience that science and mathematics teachers cannot write a letter in decent English.*' All historical periods may be for some people the worst of times and for others the best of times. The twentieth century has witnessed rapid accelerations of cultural change, and for the nostalgic temperament life becomes a kind of vertigo, a desperate longing for lost stabilities. Examples of this nostalgia from the past often read very like the sentimentalities of the present. Also in 1912 a headmaster wrote '... *parents used to read aloud to their children, and there was little trash printed. Now no-one reads aloud, and there is hardly anything printed but trash. Moreover, children now take their amusements passively. The gramophone is in the home. Children therefore come to school having hardly used their faculties at all.*' The Newbolt Report of 1921 said that:

❝ ... the chief need of business is a liberal supply of young entrants, trained to express themselves in spoken and written English with facility and correctness.... This supply, so far from being liberal, is at present almost non-existent. Our first question, 'Have you found difficulty in obtaining employees who can speak and write English clearly and correctly?' was answered with an emphatic affirmative by all but a few firms.... All complained, often bitterly, of defects in spelling, punctuation, vocabulary and sentence structure. Spelling, in particular, received adverse comment.

In 1930 Ivor Bowen, a county court judge, was quoted in *The Times* saying that '*of the people who come before me seventy-five per cent cannot read the oath and a large number cannot write or spell.*' The Norwood Report of 1943 reported: '*From all quarters, Universities, Professional Bodies, firms and business houses, training colleges and many other interests and many individuals we have received strong evidence of the poor quality of the English of Secondary School pupils ... the evidence is such as to leave no doubt in our minds that we are confronted by a serious failure of the secondary schools.*' In 1952 a Commanding Officer of an army training centre reported that some national servicemen on the station saw the same film twice in one week, only because they could not read the cinema notices that told them the name of the film. (Examples taken from *Act Now*, No. 28, Association of Christian Teachers, 2 Romeland Hill, St. Albans, Herts AL3 4ET.)

These comments, some from official reports, others just gossip, are likely to continue into the foreseeable future. Low standards make a story for the media. Old people usually believe standards are in decline. The tragedy is that the decision to rewrite the English National Curriculum, which caused so much anguish and wasted so much money, should have been influenced by this ever-popular nostalgia. There was much evidence in the early 1990s that standards in the teaching of English were improving because of the National Curriculum, and that radical change was not needed.

The fashionable view that standards were in decline was further strengthened by Kenneth Clarke when he was Secretary of State for Education. In December 1991 his Ministry leaked information to the *Mail on Sunday* saying that official statistics showed that 28 per cent of all seven-year-olds could not even recognise three letters of the alphabet, and had made no progress in reading. The *Mail on Sunday* splashed this across the front page under the headline 'Shameful'. Radio 4, Channel 4 and other newspapers repeated the story, and Clarke himself used the figures in an article for the *Daily Mail* headlined: 'For our Children's Sake, These Bureaucrats Must be Broken.'

The Department of Education later admitted that the statistics were completely false. Henrietta Dombey, a leading specialist in the teaching of reading, received an apology from Marmaduke Hussey, Chairman of the BBC, who admitted 'a serious factual error' had been made. But Hussey refused to order the BBC to broadcast a correction. As with Professor Ronald Carter over LINC, attempts to rebut damaging lies about education can do almost nothing to reduce the impact of banner headlines about a supposed decline in standards.

In the early 1990s a series of accusations about a decline in educational standards appeared in the press, presumably deliberately orchestrated by the Centre for Policy Studies and the Campaign for Real Education to support their campaign to rewrite the National Curriculum. On 9 December 1991 Sheila Lawlor published an article accusing HMI of the lion's share of responsibility for an 'extraordinary story of decline and decay' (see Trevor Dickinson for full discussion in *Made Tongue-Tied By Authority*, pp. 20–2). She said, without any evidence, that '*no longer can pupils write the clear, correct English that was second nature to their grandparents.*' Presumably their grandparents were the ones whose low standards in spelling and grammar were lambasted in the Newbolt and Norwood Reports of 1921 and 1943. She declared that '*standards have been slipping year by year, not merely despite HMI but on account of it,*' and that HMI took part in 'the defeat of grammar' in National Curriculum English. Her remarks repeat the fantasies and misrepresentations of Dr Marks's lecture. In fact as early as 1974 HMI warned against swinging the pendulum too far from the teaching teacher to the learning child. In 1984 it drew attention to the need for English teachers to pay greater attention to punctuation. In 1987 it warned about the problems of mixed-ability teaching. I met many HMI when I chaired the National Curriculum English Working Group. All took it for granted – to take two examples – that the teaching of spelling and Shakespeare were essential in the classroom. All were moderate and sensible with considerable professional knowledge of schools.

NFER reports suggest that standards of reading and writing have remained much the same in recent years. In February 1993, a report from the National Foundation for Educational Research showed that standards of spelling among secondary school children had improved markedly between 1979 and 1988. NFER researchers who studied scripts from 1,500 children aged 11 to 15 found that more than half made only one spelling error in the first ten lines, that 40 per cent of fifteen-year-olds made no mistakes and that eleven-year-olds in 1988 performed significantly better than eleven-year-olds in 1979. NFER researchers used material from a language monitoring project run by the Assessment of Performance Unit between 1979 and 1988 (see *Spelling It Out, the spelling ability of 11 and 15 year olds*, NFER, 1993). I do not suggest that this research necessarily proves that standards are improving. There are so many variables. What it does prove is that allegations that standards are set in permanent decline are nonsense.

Prince Charles

The belief that standards are in decline was repeated by Prince Charles in high-profile speeches in 1989 and 1990, and this too very much damaged the reputation of the teaching profession. I corresponded with Prince Charles in 1989, and in 1990 attended a small seminar on education he organised at his house in Highgrove. I have described this occasion in detail in my autobiography, *The Great Betrayal* (1992). On 19 December 1989, Prince Charles had given a much publicised speech when presenting the Thomas Cranmer Schools Prize. He contrasted the English of Shakespeare and the Authorised Version of the Bible with today's sloppy colloquial language in tabloids and on television. He declared that our language had become 'impoverished'. Such comparisons between language in the seventeenth and twentieth centuries (spoken or written?) are absurd, and language today is certainly not 'impoverished'. Language has not declined from some golden age in the early seventeenth century, and this is typical conservative sentimental nostalgia. In the poetry of T.S. Eliot, W.B. Yeats, Robert Lowell or Sylvia Plath, or in the fiction of D.H.Lawrence, Saul Bellow, Toni Morrison or Nadine Gordimer, among a host of major writers, literature in the twentieth century has been remarkably resilient, in spite of the competition from radio, film and television.

In his 1991 Stratford speech on the 426th anniversary of Shakespeare's birth, Prince Charles added more support to the fantasy that Shakespeare is not taught properly in schools. In fact in recent years, particularly through the influence of Rex Gibson of the Cambridge Institute of Education, the teaching of Shakespeare has probably been more stimulating and successful than ever before. When I was at secondary school in the 1940s, a few lucky pupils participated in the annual Shakespeare production rehearsed out of school hours, but the great majority in their study of Shakespeare at school never participated in any dramatic event, and indeed spent very little time considering his plays as theatrical performances.

The participants at Prince Charles's education seminar were a surprising group for such a purpose. He had invited 'a small number of people whose views on language and education he respects'. They included no teacher from state education. George Walden, a Conservative MP, was there. During the discussion he criticised the lack of idealism among teachers in state schools, to which Anne Sloman, a BBC producer, and I replied with sharp rejoinders. In subsequent years

Walden wrote articles mainly in the *Daily Telegraph* attacking the teaching profession. I was impressed by Prince Charles's sincerity and desire to improve standards, but felt he was badly advised.

Throughout this chapter I have given example after example of the extraordinary rhetoric of the right-wing group who assumed power over the National Curriculum. Walden's assertion that teachers in state schools lack idealism is akin to criticisms of the profession in Martin Turner's *Sponsored Reading Failure*. I have met hundreds of teachers in state education with the highest ideals as they work through evenings and week-ends to serve their pupils. Such abuse of teachers and the so-called educational establishment is close to hysteria, and one wonders what suppressed emotions lead to some of the wilder attacks. In the early 1990s this group created a great national fantasy that standards were in decline and teachers often incompetent. Such allegations, when repeated week by week in newspapers and on radio and television, create beliefs which facts and arguments in letters in quality newspapers can do little to dispel, and which crucially influence government policy. This was a major problem for teachers in 1993 when the rewriting of the English National Curriculum and the introduction of unsuitable tests for Key Stage 3 led to direct confrontation with the Government. Hundreds of teachers worked extraordinarily hard to sway public opinion, with some considerable success, and I shall describe their efforts in chapter 6.

3

The Warwick Evaluation of National Curriculum English

The Warwick research

In the summer of 1991 the NCC commissioned the University of Warwick to undertake, on its behalf, an evaluation of National Curriculum English. The evaluation was designed to investigate aspects of the subject's implementation in schools. It concentrated on the first three key stages (pupils aged from 5 to 14). The project team was asked to gauge '*whether any problems in implementing the English Order were the result of the Order itself, whether it was a question of teacher knowledge and understanding, or whether Statements of Attainment were pitched inappropriately for pupils in particular key stages.*' Work began in September 1991. The project was directed by Professor Bridie Raban. When the final document was released to the Press in November 1993, it was published in the names of Professor Bridie Raban, Urszula Clark and Joanna McIntyre.

The NCC decision in July 1992 to recommend to the Secretary of State that the English Order should be rewritten very much altered the context in which the Warwick evaluation took place. In the NCC document *National Curriculum English: The Case for Revising the Order*, it is said that in coming to its decision to change the Order the NCC drew upon the first interim report submitted in March 1992 by the Warwick research team. References are made to this interim report, saying that a main message from the Warwick research is that '*the programmes of study do not provide teachers with a clear, unequivocal statement about what is required in the teaching of initial reading.*' Levels 1 and 2 are said not to be defined with sufficient precision and are pitched too far apart. (This problem had been well-known for some time, and was largely due to the difficulty of defining levels 1 and 2 in relation to early reading development.) The NCC document continues: '*A further concern identified by the Warwick analysis is that more advanced reading skills need to be made more explicit. At Key Stage 2, the Order requires pupils to be "shown how to read different kinds of materials in different ways". How this should be done is not made clear.*'

This interim report from the Warwick research group was never published. The handling of the interim report by NCC in its *The Case for Revising the Order* was scandalous. The impression is given that the Warwick research strongly supported the case for revising the Order. This was not so, for two main reasons. First, the research had hardly begun. Second, the research soon showed that teachers were happy with most aspects of the current English Orders, were anxious for no more disruption and no radical changes, and felt that improvements should come solely through non-statutory advice.

From September 1991 until the end of the year, the research team spent their time analysing the current Order so that when they visited schools they could ask precise questions about specific attainment targets and programmes of study. During this period participating LEAs were identified, schools contacted, and instruments for use during fieldwork were designed and piloted. Fieldwork in schools only began in January 1992. The March interim report was based only on work during the first half of the Spring term 1992. These preliminary findings were taken from observation of sixteen classrooms for Key Stage 1 and five for Key Stage 2. The number of teacher interviews was eleven for Key Stage 1 and three for Key Stage 2. The sets of school documents inspected were three for Key Stage 1 and one for Key Stage 2, just four schools in total. The March report said: '*It should be noted that only a small number of schools provide data at this stage and any findings are very tentative and preliminary to future reports.*'

These facts *were* never made public during the great debate about revisions of the Order which took place in autumn 1992. The researchers, of course, were forced to obey rules of confidentiality. If the facts about how little research in the classroom had been completed had been generally known, the educational establishment would have found it much easier to combat the preposterous claims of the NCC case for revising the Order. This is only one of many examples of the secrecy and misinformation which the Government used at this time to prevent its policies from being questioned by independents who knew the facts. I learnt of the tentative nature of the March interim report only in December 1994, and, as far as I know, this truth has never before been published. The Warwick team submitted a further report at the end of August 1992, but the NCC July recommendations to revise the English curriculum were written and dispatched *before* this report was available; the NCC July document refers specifically to the March 1992 interim report to support its case.

And the Warwick researchers, as I have said, found strong opposition among teachers to any radical revision of the English curriculum. Their findings were leaked to the *Sunday Telegraph* on 24 May 1992 under the headline: 'Anger after dons reject return to the three Rs'. The *Sunday Telegraph* article by Fran Abrams begins: '*Plans to revive traditional methods of teaching English have been thrown into disarray after a group of academics commissioned to investigate bringing back more formal methods said there was little need for change.*' The Warwick research, Fran Abrams says, concluded that teachers already have the balance right, and appears directly to contradict education ministers who have called for a return to traditional methods: '*The former Education Secretary, Kenneth Clarke, made a return to these methods a central plank of the Government's education strategy.*'

The *Sunday Telegraph* article claims that the Warwick research was against too much emphasis on phonics in the teaching of reading, and then quotes Joyce Morris and John Bald, advocates of phonics teaching, attacking the Warwick report as 'ridiculous' because children were not 'getting the basic teaching that is necessary'. Because of confidentiality the Warwick researchers could not reply to this extraordinary travesty of their very tentative early research, and NCC did not come to their rescue. Presumably Joyce Morris and John Bald were replying to information provided by a journalist over the phone, and they could not have seen the research documentation. The leaking of this material to the ultra-Conservative *Sunday Telegraph* helped traditionalists to rubbish the Warwick research before it had come into the public domain.

Some information about the relationship between the researchers and NCC has been provided by one of them, Urszula Clark, in an article 'Bringing English to Order: a Personal Account of the NCC English Evaluation Project', published by NATE in *English Education*, Spring 1994. Her first paragraph is worded very strongly:

❦ From the beginning, working on the project commissioned by NCC to evaluate the implementation of the English Order felt like working in a dark, ever-receding tunnel, stabbing around in the vague hope that something might penetrate the blind silence and wilful obstinacy that disregarded the voice of the English teaching profession, including, it seemed, NCC itself. Trust, integrity, academic freedom: none of these appeared to be of any consequence. It was also hard to believe that personnel employed by the NCC had once been teachers, including teachers of English, themselves. Increasingly, trust between the English teaching profession and those entrusted with safeguarding its philosophy and the nature of its content was being broken.

She describes the dismay of the researchers when their confidential report was leaked to the press in May 1992, misquoted or quoted out of context. The next interim report, sent in for its due date of 31 August 1992, was also leaked to the press, with a copy sent to the *Times Educational Supplement*. Urszula Clark confirms that the researchers were never consulted by NCC when in July NCC claimed the Warwick findings supported the case for revision; she confirms also that the Warwick recommendations stated clearly that the few problems created by the 1989 English curriculum could best be addressed by further non-statutory guidance rather than by actual change in the Order.

Urszula Clark describes how the Warwick evaluation project was redirected from September 1992, immediately after the Minister announced the English curriculum would be revised. The Warwick team was asked to research the additional issues of: '*the teaching methods used to teach initial reading and writing; the manageability of the English curriculum; the teaching and sequence of progression of spelling, handwriting and more advanced reading skills; the contexts and range of literature taught at Key Stages 2 and 3 and the teaching of grammar*' (p.37). As she points out, NCC was not interested in knowledge about language, which was to be eradicated from the syllabus, only in traditional grammar. These changes in the research specification were obviously intended to provide information for a revision of the curriculum which would please the NCC traditionalists.

The Warwick researchers were continually visited by NCC professional officers, and felt that the independence of their research was under threat from NCC. The shifting requirements of NCC put great pressure on the researchers. Before September 1992, many schools had worked hard to prepare for questions from the Warwick team which were derived from the original research specifications based on the Cox curriculum. When they were asked to jettison this work and prepare for a new brief many were naturally angry, and some withdrew. But the researchers continued through all these difficulties, and in November 1993, published a splendid report of high quality. This was finally published by SCAA in 1994.

For most teachers of English the NCC case for rewriting National Curriculum English seemed perverse. Why change a highly popular Order when the research into its implementation had only just begun? Why was the interim Warwick report not published so we could judge for ourselves?

On 1 December 1992 the *TES* organised a debate on Shakespeare in the Curriculum at the Royal Theatre in London, and I was one of the speakers. At the interval I met David Pascall, the new Chair of NCC, for the first time. We chatted during the interval together with Patricia Rowan, editor of the *TES*. In this company I could not resist the temptation to ask David Pascall why the Warwick Report was not made available to the press. He promised it would be, and kept his word. The August Report was not published, but NCC conceded that interested parties might see it. Diane Hofkins, the *TES* journalist assigned to the task of writing up the research findings, rang me to say the Warwick document offered her little as a story because by and large it said that the English Order was being successfully implemented in the classroom. I replied that this was the point. The story was that there was no story, for the Warwick research did not support the NCC case for an immediate radical revision of the English curriculum. By this time it was several months since the decision to rewrite the curriculum had been headline news. Diane Hofkins did her best (11 December), but it was not a strong enough story for national newspapers to give it coverage. She explained that the cost of rewriting the curriculum was nearly £500,000, and once a new Order and supporting documents were published and distributed, the total was estimated at about £1 million. She emphasised strongly that the Warwick research showed that Ministers' demands for the English curriculum to be rewritten to bring back more traditional methods was unnecessary: '*The great books of English literature, whole-class teaching and structured approaches to the teaching of reading, with phonics at the centre, are all thriving in schools, a team from Warwick University has found.*' Unfortunately NCC had no intention of changing its mind, and by this time early drafts of the rewrite were complete.

On many occasions after the 1989 English curriculum was published I said that my Working Group had been given only one year to find solutions for all the major problems in the teaching of English language

•

and literature, and that our recommendations would need revision in the light of experience. The Warwick Report analysed weaknesses in our proposals, and made valuable recommendations for change. It is a tragedy for teachers of English and their pupils that the NCC began to revise the curriculum before this research had been completed. When the Warwick research was eventually published, it proved to be an invaluable document, based on a study of hundreds of hours observing in classrooms, interviews with teachers and analysis of school documents in many schools across England.

The Warwick Report ends with a series of conclusions and recommendations, including: '*An overriding finding is that above all else teachers felt the need for a period of stability. At Key Stages 1 and 2 in particular, the response to the proposed revision of English resulted in teachers halting any further effort in implementation*' (p.126). This devastating brief comment demonstrates the damage to the teaching of English brought about by NCC's decision to revise the English curriculum when it was still in its early stages in the classroom. Goodwill was destroyed. The work to implement a coherent English national curriculum was halted.

The Warwick Report said that '*schools and teachers at Key Stages 1, 2 and 3 were successfully using the Order in their planning and delivery of the teaching of English,*' and that '*whilst teachers acknowledged, and our evaluation has indicated, some weaknesses within the English Order, teachers have welcomed National Curriculum English as a workable framework within which their work with pupils can develop. They believe it can be strengthened best through further support and sharply targeted guidance*' (pp.124-6). The Report confirmed that the introduction of the English Order had resulted in more systematic, structured planning for the teaching of all aspects of the curriculum. Teachers commented on a greater sense of collaboration which was a feature of this planning. The Report said: '*teachers in small primary schools benefited from planning the English curriculum through liaison with colleagues in other schools.*' This fulfilled one of the prime objectives of those who advocated a National Curriculum. Schools were persuaded to plan their teaching in accordance with a blueprint which reflected the best professional advice on the teaching of English.

For Key Stages 1 and 2 there was general agreement that primary school teachers were happy with the content of the Order. Any difficulties in implementing it were said to be due to lack of time to deliver all the requirements of the other eight subject Orders. This question of excessive workload became a major issue in 1993, when Sir

Ron Dearing addressed himself specifically to this problem. I summarise the main findings of the Warwick Report under five headings: reading, literature, writing, knowledge about language, and speaking and listening. The descriptions by the researchers of what was really happening in classrooms bears little relation to what was being said at the time in tabloid newspapers.

Reading

In learning to read at Key Stage 1, phonics activities were the ones which pupils experienced most often and for the longest time. Another common activity, used frequently by teachers to teach reading, was listening to pupils read. However, hearing reading was time-consuming. To cope with this, teachers set their classes a variety of independent reading activities, such as phonic work, or repetition and practice activities, thereby releasing themselves to hear individual pupils read. The researchers wrote: '*In teaching reading, teachers used a wide range of activities in the early stages. Their planning for teaching phonics was structured and followed a sequence of progression through checklists and published schemes.*' Teachers most often used a combination of reading schemes, supplemented by books from class or school libraries. Those schools that used a range of books not tied to any published scheme had adopted or devised a graded scheme, such as 'colour-coding', that allowed them to monitor and assess pupils' progress, as well as to guide pupils in their choice of books. Teachers increasingly used published reading programmes to monitor progress between levels 1 and 2. This summary of common practice in schools brings out how grossly exaggerated were claims in the press that teachers did not use phonics or structured programmes of work in the teaching of reading.

At Key Stage 1 the teachers were successful in implementing the requirements of the National Curriculum, but the researchers discovered problems for teachers of reading at Key Stage 2. There was a need for a more consistent match between the Statements of Attainment and the Programmes of Study in this area. The researchers concluded: '*The Order does not provide an appropriate developmental framework for More Advanced Reading Skills, nor does it give sufficiently clear emphasis to the development of More Advanced Reading Skills at Key Stage 2*' (p. 124). The gaps between levels 1 and 2 in Reading and Writing were found by teachers to be too wide. The difficulty was that level 2 was too broad.

Teachers felt that these problems should be first addressed by non-statutory guidance, and certainly not by a complete rewrite of the curriculum.

Literature

At Key Stage 2 teachers placed greater emphasis on developing the habit of reading by providing time for pupils to read individually and hear stories read rather than on teaching particular texts. Teachers incorporated teaching about literary texts into topic work wherever they felt that was appropriate. Reading literary texts or extracts from literary texts was often used as a stimulus for discussion and creative writing, rather than to study the texts themselves. Teachers recommended a wide range of titles, mainly from the modern period (post-1941) with some additional titles from pre- and early twentieth-century literature. Key Stage 3 teachers also recommended an extensive range and variety of texts, including poetry and prose in addition to dramatic texts, which were given more emphasis than at Key Stage 2. Teachers for Key Stage 3 also most commonly recommended post-1941 titles, though they too guided their pupils towards pre- and early twentieth-century texts. Many teachers have told me that after 1989 they took more care to ensure that pupils read some pre-1900 literature.

This work was undermined by the introduction of the Key Stage 3 Standard Assessment Tasks (SATs) for 1993. Heads of Department said that this forced them to abandon schemes of work for Year 9, and to teach to the test rather than to the curriculum (see chapter 6 for discussion of the Key Stage 3 problems of 1993).

Writing

At Key Stage 1 the teaching of Writing was seen to be in accordance with the recommendations of the Order and directed specifically towards the requirements of Key Stage 1 tests. The teaching strategies for Handwriting in the Order were put into practice at Key Stage 1, but this was not the case at Key Stage 2, where there was need for teaching practice to catch up with school policy documents based on the National Curriculum requirements. The National Curriculum had changed teaching practice by persuading schools to teach cursive writing at an earlier age than previously, and to target lessons in handwriting for groups or the whole class rather than individuals, which had previously been the case. The researchers observed in the classoom, however, that teachers frequently monitored and taught handwriting on an individual basis. In both handwriting and spelling the National Curriculum had necessitated a more formal, structured approach than previously, and this reflects what my Working Group hoped would happen. As pupils progressed through the Key Stages, teachers were more likely to teach spelling using explicit teaching methods.

Knowledge about Language

Not surprisingly, the innovations of the National Curriculum were causing teachers some difficulty, and there was a need for more non-statutory guidance. Most schools had not yet established a common policy for teaching knowledge about language. The researchers found that the Order offered a practical framework for the teaching of knowledge about language, but that teachers found the Order unhelpful '*when they tried to establish terms of reference for the phrase knowledge about language*' (p.125). At Key Stage 1 teachers perceived knowledge about language, particularly grammar and punctuation in writing, to form part of their teaching of English. Observation in classrooms and activities recorded by teachers showed that these teachers taught about the organisation and use of written language related to whole texts. Teaching knowledge about language involved teaching about the conventions of written forms such as the title pages of books, writing and reading left to right and about narrative sequencing. This was interrelated with teaching pupils how to decode print and write letters, words, sentences and complete texts for themselves. Such teaching occurred as part of an ongoing activity, rather than separately, at this Key Stage. When I read this section of the Warwick Report I was particularly pleased. My English Working Group had considered making knowledge about language a separate profile component, but we decided this could make it an arid, pedantic exercise, and that children would find study of language most exciting and rewarding when it was introduced as part of their ongoing activities in writing and reading.

Teachers at both Key Stages 2 and 3 reported that they were beginning to structure their teaching about language in a more formal and explicit way since the introduction of the Order. Teachers taught about the organisation and use of language (especially grammar and punctuation) related to words and sentences as well as within longer texts. They either integrated teaching about language into the current topic of a lesson or taught it as the main focus of a lesson to a whole class. In addition, teachers taught about punctuation and sentence structure in pupils' writing by individual consultation, correcting errors and recommending improvements.

At Key Stage 3 activities concerning knowledge about language were more wide-ranging than at Key Stage 2. Teachers taught about the organisation and use of language, especially grammar and punctuation, within printed texts as well as within pupils' own written language. Teachers were also beginning to teach pupils about the theoretical aspects of language required by the attainment targets. This renewed interest in language was jeopardised in 1992 by government interference. One purpose of this book is to encourage good teachers to continue with this approach to language study. The sad truth about the determination of NCC in 1992 to introduce more grammar into the curriculum is that their old-fashioned prescriptions may in fact lead to a reaction among pupils and teachers *against* the teaching of grammar.

Speaking and Listening

The teaching of Speaking and Listening had been directly influenced by the requirements of the Order rather than by assessment demands. At Key Stages 1, 2 and 3 the most frequently encountered activity was the teacher talking to the whole class, with the pupils listening. The second most frequent category was pupils engaged in activities individually or in groups, where talk could be part of the process of the activity. When discussion took place it was mainly *with* the teacher, and most commonly directed *by* the teacher. The most common type of talk observed by the Warwick researchers involved the teacher asking closed questions (ie questions to which there was an established answer in the teacher's mind) in a teacher-directed discussion. In Key Stage 3 schools, changes in the assessment arrangements by SEAC raised doubts about the status of Speaking and Listening (see chapter 6). In these schools there was a wide variety of other types of talk than was observed at either Key Stage 1 or 2.

The recommendations at the end of the Warwick Report said that teachers would welcome examples of practice which was tried and tested in classrooms. My Working Group had considered whether we should prepare a series of examples of good practice, including examples of pupils' writing appropriate to specific levels. We abandoned this project because we had insufficient time. This is the kind of guidance (and some work was completed) which in the 1990s would have been of more benefit to schools than a complete rewrite of the curriculum. The Warwick Report's final recommendation was as follows: '*The pace of change needs to be slowed down, allowing time for a period of stability during which teachers can make professional decisions about the best ways of planning and teaching English in the National Curriculum*' (p.127). From 1992 onwards NCC and SEAC made this impossible.

A Misleading Case for Revising English

The NCC review of the English Order

After the takeover by right-wingers in the summer of 1991, it took several months of argument before the independent members of NCC could be cajoled to agree to revise the English curriculum. In July 1992 NCC forwarded *National Curriculum English: the Case for Revising the Order* to John Patten, the Secretary of State for Education. In his covering letter of 15 July, David Pascall recommended that a formal review of the English Order should be put in hand as soon as possible. The objective, he said, should be to introduce a revised Order for Key Stages 1 - 3 in September 1994, and in September 1995 for Key Stage 4. A triumph for the teachers' campaign of 1993 was that this programme for Key Stages 1 - 3 was delayed by one year, and so the Cox curriculum was actually in use in schools for six years, from 1989 to 1995. In September John Patten announced that he had accepted NCC's advice to revise the Statutory Order for National Curriculum English. In his letter to David Pascall of 9 September, he says he has noted NCC's view that the current Orders:

◆ place insufficient emphasis on the requirement that all pupils should become confident users of Standard English;
◆ do not define with sufficient precision the skills involved in learning to read, nor provide a clear and balanced framework to support the teaching of reading;

◆ are not sufficiently explicit about how pupils can develop the habit
   of reading widely, and be introduced to the richness of great
   literature;
◆ do not define clearly the basic writing skills and grammatical
   knowledge pupils need to master, and the varieties of ways in which
   competence in spelling can be developed.

Anyone with a modicum of intelligence who has read the Cox Report
will find these criticisms astonishing. They had been bred from the
fantasy land of the Centre for Policy Studies.

The decision of 9 September ended a period of rumours and
leaked stories about how NCC was considering whether to commence a
review of the English Order two or three years ahead of the schedule
originally laid down in 1989. In a pamphlet published by NATE in
November 1992, *Made Tongue-Tied by Authority: New Orders for English?*,
John Johnson, Research Officer for NATE, wrote of the period up to
summer 1992:

❝ A number of politicians, political lobbyists such as the Centre for
  Policy Studies, and members of the NCC Council itself appeared to be
  manipulating the media to create a suitable atmosphere in which to
  unveil a new agenda for English teaching. Yet their collective
  discussions and manoeuvrings took place in a semi-secret world from
  which teachers, parents, pupils and others concerned with education
  are largely excluded - the corridors of the DFE, NCC and SEAC. Most
  teachers, LEAs and specialist associations such as the National
  Association for the Teaching of English, were forced to rely on press
  accounts, and whatever they could glean from DFE officials, to find
  out what was happening. (p.3)

Full details of a letter from Lord Brian Griffiths to government advisers
were leaked on 7 June 1992 in the *Sunday Times*. This letter condemned
the Cox curriculum as 'imprecise and woolly', and criticised the failure
to lay down exactly what children need to know about grammar,
punctuation and spelling. According to the *Sunday Times* report, he
wrote: '*English is such a crucial part of the National Curriculum, revision
should be started as soon as possible.*' In the same newspaper report Martin
Turner appeared as '*an educational psychologist who has exposed a fall in
reading standards in the 1980s*', who says the English curriculum has been
influenced by 'fads' and 'fashions'.

This well-orchestrated abuse of the Cox curriculum was repeated by
John Patten in a speech on 12 June 1992, to his Oxford West and
Abingdon constituency association. He said that emphasis on good

grammar and spelling must be strengthened, and that he was not convinced the Government had got the teaching of English right. Progressive approaches to English teaching, he said, were the most stark example of a 'soft-headed' attitude undermining the education system, and he would not hesitate to make further changes in the National Curriculum if necessary.

I have talked to Civil Servants who were advising Mr. Patten during this period. They strongly urged him not to revise the English curriculum for three good reasons:

◆ the English curriculum had proved popular, and there was as yet insufficient time since its inception to assess its strengths and weaknesses;

◆ a decision to revise the English curriculum would be extremely damaging to teacher morale, for teachers had expended great time and effort in implementing the 1989 programmes of study;

◆ in many cases, teachers would immediately stop their work to implement the 1989 curriculum, and all the good work to raise standards would be interrupted.

This advice was confirmed by the Warwick research. When in 1994 I drew the attention of one of the Civil Servants to this research, he replied that it was pleasant to find that research confirmed what in 1992 was obvious common sense.

Before July 1992, when NCC published its case for revising the English Order, many examples of misguided interference in the English assessment process by Lord Griffiths had already taken place. In his NATE article John Johnson wrote that in the previous fifteen months SEAC and NCC had been used more as political agents than as educational bodies. New rules had been repeatedly set for assessment at seven, eleven, fourteen and sixteen, often creating administrative chaos for schools and examination boards. In English, new narrow tests for seven-year-olds for spelling and group reading comprehension were widely condemned as pedagogically unsound. Johnson wrote: '*Different criteria were imposed on the assessment of seven-year-olds' writing, with which schools strongly disagreed. They have caused standards to deteriorate nationally*' (p.4). The introduction of new GCSE syllabuses had brought a continuous flow into schools of amendments, alterations, corrections and extensions as SEAC changed the rules on almost a weekly basis.

The decisions leading to this chaos seem to have been made largely by Lord Griffiths himself, against professional advice. At that time I was lecturing almost every week to groups of English teachers. They could not contain their anger at the incompetence of SEAC which was ruining their carefully-prepared programmes of work based on the 1989 English curriculum. In my lectures I repeatedly said that the attempt by the Centre for Policy Studies to impose curriculum and assessment changes against the professional advice of almost every good teacher in the country could lead only to ill-will and chaos. At a seminar in Lincolnshire a primary school teacher said to me that whatever NCC or SEAC decided he would always do what he thought best for the pupils in his classroom. He had no other criterion. This idealism among school teachers meant that the Centre for Policy Studies' programme for change would never be properly implemented, and would inevitably create confusion with damage to standards.

NCC's *National Curriculum English: the Case for Revising the Order* was a carefully written document which acknowledged the validity of some objections to the rewriting of the Order, and yet claimed, with a minimum of evidence, that the balance of argument from informed sources was in favour of revision. The document admitted that the 1989 curriculum had strengths, and that a revision could damage teacher morale. These objections were set aside. I have already described the misuse of the Warwick research to support the case for revision.

Replies to the NCC Case for Revising English

In the autumn a series of essays appeared pointing out the omissions, mistakes and misrepresentations of the NCC document. I contributed essays to the *Guardian* ('Curriculum for Chaos', 15 September), The *Times* (the headline read: 'Brian Cox argues that generations of children have been betrayed by political dogma', 21 September) and the *TES* ('Keep faith in the English revolution', 25 September). My autobiography, *The Great Betrayal,* was published in September, so at least the NCC helped my book to gain maximum publicity in newspapers, radio and television. It's an ill wind....

To liven up my *Guardian* article I ended by repeating a persistent rumour, which I had heard from two senior Civil Servants, that the Prime Minister had allowed his extreme right-wingers to take over the education agenda on the understanding that they would go quiet in their opposition to the Maastricht treaty. I said I had no idea if this was true, but it fitted the situation which had emerged in the previous months. Later I had some regrets about repeating this rumour. It was quoted everywhere, and for many people took on historical validity.

The threat of a radical revision of the English curriculum was discussed at NATE's annual conference in Birmingham in April 1992. Discussions between NATE officers and officers of the National Association of Advisers in English led to a joint survey of sixteen LEAs, conducted by a small team from both organisations. The survey investigated the implementation of English in the National Curriculum in schools. The Report of the survey, based on responses from one-sixth of all LEAs, was published on 26 May 1992. It was sent to NCC, to DFE officials and to HMI. This Report was listed by NCC in its *The Case for Revising the Order* as one of the documents consulted. Not surprisingly, the NCC failed to quote the many statements in this Report which demonstrate how successfully the English curriculum was being implemented in schools. The main findings of the survey were listed by John Johnson in his Introduction to NATE's *Made Tongue-Tied by Authority*. Here are a few of the most salient:

◆ In 'Speaking and Listening', the National Curriculum had led to:
    (a) improvements in teachers' planning and children's work;
    (b) improved methods of assessment.
◆ In 'Reading':
    (a) teachers' understanding of how children learn to read has improved;
    (b) the range of reading in the classroom has been extended;
    (c) almost all teachers used a range of methods for teaching reading, including phonics.
◆ In 'Writing':
    (a) increasing challenges and demands were being made of children as writers;
    (b) a greater range of tasks was being set;
    (c) basic writing skills were receiving satisfactory attention;
    (d) writing skills seemed to be best developed in the context of pupils' own writing.
◆ In 'Spelling, Handwriting and Presentation':
    (a) many schools had improved their policies for and teaching of spelling and handwriting;
    (b) handwriting had been given a higher priority since the Order.
◆ In 'Knowledge about Language':
    (a) knowledge about language was being given a higher profile in the classroom;
    (b) there was more English teaching of grammatical terminology.

The survey revealed the English Order had led to considerable improvements in the writing and introduction of proper schemes of work, and of systems for recording and assessing pupils' progress. There was increased rigour, thoroughness and accountability in teachers' work in English. The survey concluded that a rewrite would have a devastating effect on teachers' morale and sense of professionalism, and would be more likely to lower standards than to raise them.

This Report shows once again the frightening contrast between reality and pronouncements about classrooms from associates of the Centre for Policy Studies. It also shows how spectacularly inaccurate were the criticisms of the English curriculum in the Secretary of State's letter of 9 September.

NCC misrepresentations

In *Made Tongue-Tied by Authority*, Pat Barrett, before 1992 the Professional Officer for English at the NCC, described the shock she felt when she compared the criticisms of the Cox Report in the NCC July document with her knowledge of what was really happening. As NCC Professional Officer she had been involved in preparing hour-long tapes and interview schedules in different schools on the implementation of the English curriculum. None of this had been published. Nothing was ever published because the information directly contradicted the assertions made by NCC in July 1992. In her article she compared examples of the NCC criticisms with what was actually said in the 1989 Statutory Orders for English. She gave clear examples of misrepresentation. Here are some instances:

Standard English

The NCC document when dealing with 'Speaking and Listening' in the Cox curriculum said:

❝ The one explicit reference to Standard English in the Statements of Attainment focuses on the need to develop 'an awareness of grammatical differences between spoken Standard English and a non-standard variety'. This is not the same thing as being able to use Standard English in conversation and will not necessarily encourage pupils to speak clearly, accurately and confidently. There is a case, therefore, for strengthening the references to the mastery of Standard

English in the Statements of Attainment and Programmes of Study, and, more specifically, for requiring children to use Standard English before level 5.

These sentences gave an entirely false impression of what the Cox Report says about Standard English. They were quoted in several newspapers without comment. The reason why there is only one reference is because at the head of the attainment target there is the following blanket requirement: '*From level 7, pupils should be using Standard English, wherever appropriate, to meet the Statements of Attainment.*' In the Programmes of Study for Key Stage 3 and 4 for 'Speaking and Listening' there are several references to Standard English, for example: '*In order to achieve level 6, pupils should be guided towards the use of spoken Standard English in public or formal situations.... It is important that pupils working towards level 7 and beyond have increasing opportunities to use spoken Standard English, and in particular that those who do not speak it as a native dialect should be helped to extend their language competence so that they can use Standard English with confidence.*' The Cox Report, of course, included a whole chapter explaining the rationale behind our proposals for teaching Standard English.

Listening

On the importance of Listening the NCC document said:

> There is, in addition, the question of whether the Order pays sufficient attention to listening skills. Oral communication depends as much on the ability to listen as it does on the ability to express one's views. At present, the ability to listen is identified in levels 1 - 3, but from level 4 onwards the Statements of Attainment concentrate on the pupil's ability to articulate information and ideas and explicit references to listening skills are given less prominence.

This too gave a false impression. Level 4 in the attainment target for 'Speaking and Listening' in the 1989 curriculum included the following two requirements:

(*a*) ask and respond to questions in a range of situations with increased confidence;

(*b*) take part as speakers and listeners in a group discussion or activity, expressing a personal view and commenting constructively on what is being discussed or experienced.

Level 5 includes:
> contribute to and respond constructively in discussion, including the development of ideas; advocate and justify a point of view.

Level 6 includes:
> contribute, to group discussions, considered opinions or clear statements of personal feeling which are clearly responsive to the contributions of others.

Level 7 includes:
> express a point of view clearly and cogently to a range of audiences, and interpret accurately a range of statements by others.

Level 8 includes:
> (a) express points of view on complex matters clearly and cogently and interpret points of view with accuracy and discrimination.
>
> (b) take an active part in group discussions, contributing constructively to the sustained development of the argument.

Level 9 includes:
> take an active part in group discussion, displaying sensitivity, listening critically and being self-critical.

Level 10 includes:
> take a variety of leading roles in group discussion, including taking the chair, listening with concentration and understanding and noting down salient points.

The references to response and listening here show that the NCC document was seriously misleading. I have quoted them at length to show why educationalists felt such rage at the NCC's blatant trafficking with the truth to support the determination to rewrite the curriculum. I presume that some members of NCC wanted children to spend more time passively listening to the teacher, and that is why the emphasis on response did not please them.

The same falsifications occurred in the NCC comments on Spelling. The NCC document said that the 1989 curriculum placed too much emphasis on teaching spelling in the context of the children's own writing: '*While useful work can and should be done through attention to what the child has written, there are other classroom activities which can involve children in an enthusiastic manner and help develop their spelling ability. The Order makes no reference to any such activities.*' The last sentence was simply untrue. In the 1989 English Curriculum Programmes of Study for Key Stage 3 appeared the following two recommendations:

(a) pupils should be helped to recognise, in the context of their own writing and reading, that words with related meanings may have related spellings and that this can sometimes be an aid in the spelling of words where the sound alone does not provide sufficient information;

(b) pupils should learn, in the context of their own writing and reading, some of the words and roots which have been absorbed into English from other languages, so that they become familiar with the word-building process and spelling patterns that derive from them.

In her article Pat Barrett provided eleven examples of this kind of misrepresentation, with lots of brief quotations comparing the NCC document with the words of the 1989 curriculum. I have given fuller details of both documents for a few examples so readers who are unfamiliar with the 1989 curriculum can see why the NCC document misled many politicians and journalists. When responding to journalists I found myself often being asked questions such as: '*Surely you agree that the National Curriculum should emphasise the importance of spelling and Standard English?*' I had to explain that the 1989 curriculum already fulfilled these requirements.

After the Secretary of State's decision on 9 September 1992 to allow NCC to rewrite the English curriculum, a whole series of major documents were sent to NCC showing that its arguments were fallacious, would damage standards and were in opposition to research and good teaching practice. NCC responded to some specific criticisms, such as the need to define Standard English more sensibly, but in the autumn and winter of 1992-3 otherwise ignored the great weight of professional advice so carefully prepared by teachers and educationalists. Some members of NCC, of course, regarded the teaching profession as an enemy to be resisted.

The NUT response

The response from the National Union of Teachers covered 23 pages with 117 paragraphs. It found the case against revision 'overwhelming'. The response incorporated a thorough analysis of all major issues about English teaching, with devastating arguments about the folly of revising the curriculum at such an early stage in its development: '*the Union can see no good reason for such a course of action.*' The NUT arguments, of course, were almost entirely ignored.

The NCC's Corporate Plan for 1992-3 had insisted that the curriculum must not be driven by assessment issues. The NUT response referred to this, and drew attention to Lord Griffiths's letter leaked in June 1992 to the *Sunday Times* arguing that revision of English should start as soon as possible. The NUT replied to Lord Griffiths:

❢ The Union is not aware of any analysis conducted or commissioned by SEAC of any possible difficulties for assessment posed by the English Attainment Target levels. Nor is it aware of any calls from teachers who have conducted the Key Stage 1 English Standard Assessment Tasks, or who were involved in trialling the Key Stage 3 English SATs, for the English Subject Order to be changed. The statement in the 'Case for Revision' that the 'Council has examined assessment difficulties in English, which have been raised by SEAC' leads the Union to question why SEAC has not chosen to make public the nature of its concerns.

The NUT response said that there was a consensus about the popularity of the English curriculum: '*the consensus around the Subject Order is not the product of compromise, but of ownership of the synthesis of the best thinking about the teaching of English. The sense of ownership is felt by all those who teach English.*'

The Union demanded that all research should be published and open to public scrutiny. I find it particularly frightening that in a democracy NCC was allowed for crucial periods of time to keep research secret, such as the Warwick findings, which were germane to its decisions and to the consultations which it was obliged by law to institute with teachers. These were educational matters of great importance to the nation's children, not plans for secret weapons or military strategies. The NUT response concluded: '*The implication of "The Case for Revising the Order" is that there is a consensus for statutory change of the Order. In the Union's view, no such consensus exists.*'

NUT objections were duplicated in submissions from many teacher and advisory groups from all over the country. The Language and Literacy team of the Primary Education Department and the Department of In-Service and Professional Development at the University of Brighton wrote to NCC:

❢ The document's definition of Standard English as 'the grammatically correct language used in formal communication throughout the world' is misleading.... It is quite simply fallacious to state that to become competent users of any language variety pupils need 'to be taught to recognise its characteristics and the rules which govern its usage'. As Chomsky showed us over 25 years ago, in learning language from the earliest stages children are constructing increasingly complex theories to give ever closer accounts of the language heard around them (N. Chomsky, *Aspects of the Theory of Syntax*, 1965). But the vast majority of such knowledge is tacit: most English-speaking children of four, for example, have a sound (if over-regularised) command of three categories of past tense in English. But they cannot, of course, begin to talk about verbs, or tense systems. By means of such tacit rule construction, learners take on new forms and new varieties of language as they are exposed to them and as they see a social need to do so (see C.G. Wells, *Language through Interaction*, 1985). At later stages in their learning (perhaps from Key Stage 2 onwards) children are increasingly able to formulate and to some extent heed explicitly stated rules. But this is not the chief means by which they extend and refine their linguistic repertoires.

This reads somewhat like an introductory textbook, but such basic information was clearly what some NCC members urgently needed. For teachers it was disturbing to watch the ease with which future NCC documents shrugged off all research and informed opinion about language acquisition, such as these Brighton comments on the development of children's language abilities. Prejudice was allowed to hold sway. The Brighton document continued by pointing out that research had shown that where reading standards were declining it was almost always not the fault of teaching methodology, but of worsening social conditions of a growing proportion of the age group. A submission from Dorset advisers similarly claimed that NCC was deliberately responding to sensational material in the media about falling standards, trendy progressives in the teaching profession and weak GCSE Boards, and that the NCC's proposals were an insult to the profession.

Professor Perera's letter

In my Introduction I described Professor Katharine Perera as an invaluable member of my Working Group who combined extensive teaching experience in the classroom with an international reputation for research into children's learning. I wrote to David Pascall to suggest that he should consult her. As a result, Richard Knott, one of NCC's professional officers, asked her to give 'advice, guidance and evidence on a range of issues in connection with the revision of the English Order'. I urged David Pascall to invite her to London to meet him so he could hear the views of perhaps the leading expert in England on National Curriculum English. He never issued an invitation, and my understanding is that during the months when the new curriculum was being drafted he was obdurate in refusing professional advice. I end this chapter with a long excerpt from a letter of 25 October she sent to Richard Knott dealing with NCC's misunderstandings of Standard English, the arguments for not changing the statements of attainment for 'Writing', and the importance of knowledge about language. Professor Perera wrote:

> '1(a) Spoken and written Standard English
> The rules that govern spoken Standard English, are in some respects, different from the rules that govern written Standard English. In the National Curriculum document, *The Case for Revising the Order*, the following statement is made about spoken Standard English (p. 4, para. 11).
>
>> 'The phrase "Standard English" refers to the grammatically correct language used in formal communication throughout the world.'
>
> It is not being merely pedantic to say that this can only be properly evaluated if we know what is meant by 'grammatically correct language'. If it means 'language that would be correct if it was produced in formal writing', then the statement is simply wrong. I will very briefly outline five ways in which the structure of spoken Standard English differs from the structure of written Standard English.
>
> (i) Most obviously, spontaneous speech contains hesitations, false starts, repetitions and incomplete utterances. These are a natural and inescapable result of the nature of the production of spontaneous speech. Speech without these features sounds unnatural: it sounds rehearsed or insincere or foreign.
> (ii) Further, spontaneous speech contains 'discourse markers' of a kind which do not occur in writing, eg *well,, sort of, you know, like, I mean*, etc. These are a very important aspect of the interpersonal nature of speech. Speakers who do not use any of them in face-to-face conversation sound as if they are lecturing their listeners rather than engaging in a co-operative activity.

(iii) Then there are some grammatical constructions which look odd written down but which are perfectly normal in the speech of educated speakers, eg

It was good, that film.

The firm that did your kitchen extension for you, did they have their own architect?

These constructions with 'redundant' pronouns help not only the speaker's production but also the listener's reception processes. (Typically, written language is more 'dense' than spoken language, which is why it can be hard to understand when read aloud.)

(iv) Spontaneous spoken language does not typically consist of a sequence of **sentences** (which are units of the grammar of writing) but rather of sequences of **clauses**. For this reason, transcripts of speech are extremely difficult to punctuate using the conventions of written language.

(v) Face-to-face spoken language typically contains elliptical utterances and references to the situational context which would be incomprehensible if they were decontextualised by being written down. If a speaker always uses full utterances and is linguistically explicit about things that are present in the situation, he or she sounds either pompous or even socially/mentally abnormal.

I cannot emphasise strongly enough that these spoken features that would not occur in writing (apart from in representations of speech) are not grammatical errors. Transcripts of the speech of any competent, articulate, educated, adult middle-class speakers will reveal all of these features and more.

There is widespread misunderstanding about the nature of spoken language. It is essential that the National Curriculum in English does not use any form of words that could foster such misunderstanding.

Another statement in the same paragraph in *The Case for Revising the Order* is the following:

'These requirements (for children to use Standard English before level 5) need to be based on a clear definition of Standard English.'

I am not indulging in an academic cavil when I say that there is no clear and straightforward definition of what **spoken** Standard English is. I have tried to show that it can't be equated with written Standard English.

Nor should it be equated solely with formal English. (Note that, if it were, this would lead to the absurdity that speakers such as members of the Royal Family and Government ministers would have to be considered to be speaking non-standard English when they were chatting with friends, for example.) It is true to say that it is a form of language that does not have many noticeably **regional** features in its grammar and vocabulary (although the pronunciation of Standard English can be in any accent), so long as the definition is confined to Standard **Southern British** English (Standard Scottish and Irish English are a bit different and Standard American English displays a number of grammatical and particularly lexical differences). But there is a very small number of grammatical constructions which are widespread throughout Britain, and not capable of being misunderstood, which nevertheless are not considered to be part of Standard English. Examples are:

> *Do you need them books?*
> *He won't never help nobody.*
> *We was listening to the radio.*

These are not part of a regional variety of English but of a working class variety. So, a first step towards a 'definition' of spoken Standard Southern British English would be:

> 'a group of varieties of English (because it must encompass formal and informal, specialist and general, for example) spoken by educated, middle-class speakers in England and Wales and widely understood.'

Quite apart from the fact that this raises the difficult questions of how 'educated' and 'middle-class' are to be defined, I am absolutely convinced that this is not an acceptable definition to include in the National Curriculum: the whole issue of social class is too sensitive and too open to misinterpretation and misrepresentation.

(b) Acquiring spoken Standard English
Paragraph 11 of *The Case for Revising the Order* states:

> 'To become competent users of standard English, pupils need to be taught to recognise its characterisics and the rules which govern its usage.'

This is not true, as far as **spoken** English is concerned, for middle-class children. They learn it as their mother tongue without any explicit teaching. None of us learns to speak our mother tongue by learning rules.

'There is a case for strengthening the references to the mastery of Standard English in the Statements of Attainment and Programmes of Study and, more specifically, for requiring children to use standard English before level 5.'

This is a most alarming suggestion for a number of reasons:

(i) it gives too much weight to the form of speech and, in doing so, undervalues articulateness, clarity, comprehensibility, organisation, communciative effectiveness, etc, etc. In other words, a 13-year-old pupil could retell a story fluently, coherently and in a way that engaged the attention of his listeners and still be accorded a level of attainment that was below his chronological age if he said, for example, 'They was...' In contrast, another 13-year-old might be tedious and uninteresting and yet be accorded a higher level simply because he had been born into a middle-class family.

(ii) It is much harder to change one's habitual pattern of speech than to adopt different grammatical structures in writing, because there is more time to reflect on and alter written language. That is why the Cox Report very deliberately and carefully specified that children should begin to show such mastery of **written** Standard English before they were expected to show such mastery in speech. For children who don't speak Standard English at home [and they are the only ones who matter in connection with this part of the Order], one of the main ways of absorbing the structures of Standard English is through reading. They must be allowed enough time as fluent and competent readers to acquire Standard English structures before they have to alter their speech patterns.

(iii)Changing one's speech patterns is not basically a linguistic matter but a social one. In other words, there is generally no problem in comprehending non-standard English; the only reason for requiring Standard English is that non-standard is socially stigmatised. Pupils need to be old enough, and mature enough, to understand the needs of the adult world before they are in a position to take what may be the difficult step of choosing to speak in a different way from their family and community. Further, for the teaching situation to be realistic there need to be contexts set up within the classroom for the requirement to use

Standard English to be a reasonable one: examples would be mock job interviews, television panel discussions, public meetings. Such contexts are not part of the normal primary classroom. (Note that it is not possible to **force** anyone to speak Standard English. The task is hard enough anyway; if pupils don't want to change, or don't see any reason for doing so, there is no chance they will successfully master spoken Standard English.)

(iv) Whatever the Order says, there will be many pupils who leave school not speaking Standard English - because the social and emotional costs of abandoning the language of home and family are too high. It is surely unacceptable that such pupils should be accorded no more than a level 3 or 4 if in all other respects their spoken English is admirable.

(v) According too high a value to spoken Standard English at too early an age would do more than anything else in the education system to discriminate against working class and ethnic minority children and their schools. The assessment would not be of teaching or learning or effort or attainment but solely of social class.

2 Writing: the amalgamation of ATs 3, 4 and 5

In *The Case for Revising the Order*, p. 6, para. 24, there is the following statement

'the ability "to construct and convey meaning" (in writing)... depends on the mastery of the basic skill of handwriting and upon the ability to spell and to write grammatically.'

This is both an overstatement and an understatement. It is an overstatement because conveying meaning in written language does not **depend** on mastery of handwriting and spelling. Most obviously, young children use word processing programs with concept keyboards and are in this way able to produce excellent written language without having learnt to form any letter shapes at all. Similarly, it is possible for spellings to be inaccurate and still to be readily comprehensible; for example, in your letter to me both my Christian name and my surname were misspelt but that didn't cause me any difficulties of comprehension.

It is an understatement because the skilful and effective conveying of meaning in writing requires a great deal more than accurate handwriting, spelling and grammar: it is possible to write neatly, spell correctly and write grammatically and still produce writing that is unclear, turgid and boring.

The crucial point is that the three aspects of writing (composing, handwriting and spelling) are logically separable. A writer may excel in any one aspect and be mediocre in the other two. That is why the original Cox Report presented these aspects of writing in separate attainment targets and I am still convinced that that is the best thing to do. If there is a fear that insufficient weight is given to spelling and handwriting, then it would always be possible to adjust the weighting between the targets. That would be preferable to conflating them within one target. The flaw with conflation is that it means the pupil will only achieve the level of his or her weakest area of performance in writing. (Logically, it would entail marking down a writer like Lawrence or Hopkins because his handwriting was poor.) This fails to achieve one of the National Curriculum's most valuable objectives, namely that reporting of pupils' performance should be maximally informative. There will be pupils who have very neat handwriting and who can spell very well - skills much sought after by some employers - who nevertheless lack the imagination or aptitude to write at a level that would achieve a GCSE grade C, for example; it would be unfortunate if a revision of the Order meant that their abilities could no longer be separately recognised.

It is also the case that, if the three aspects are kept separate, it is possible to identify those schools in a given catchment area that are doing particularly well in teaching spelling, for example. It then becomes feasible to examine their teaching methods to discover the source of their success.

3 Knowledge about language and understanding of grammar

Here, it is necessary first and foremost to consider the purpose of teaching pupils explicitly about language. The strong message that comes through *The Case for Revising the Order* is that such teaching is necessary in order for pupils to speak and write English properly. What matters is the kind of subject matter that is envisaged and the ways in which it is to be presented to pupils. There is a very substantial body of research evidence which demonstrates that the teaching of grammatical structures and terminology in isolation from the normal classroom work of reading and writing has no beneficial effects whatsoever on schoolchildren's writing. This research numbers scores of studies, conducted in the UK, the US, Australia and New Zealand with hundreds of children over the last 70 years. Various grammatical frameworks have been used; some of the researchers have set out hoping to find that a particular model of grammar enhances performance, but even they have had to report negative results.

(I can provide a list of some of these studies if necessary.)

I am a linguist and I spend much of my professional life teaching English grammar to students - which I enjoy very much. I would dearly love to be able to say that it should be taught to all secondary pupils, but I know that teaching terminology in isolation from meaningful English activities to pupils of that age has no positive effects, alienates some pupils and wastes precious lesson time.

On the other hand, a broader-based Knowledge about Language syllabus enables pupils to reflect explicitly and systematically on the differences between spoken and written language, on the nature and purposes of Standard English, on the reasons for and consequences of linguistic change, and so on. In the course of doing this kind of work they necessarily learn a great deal about the grammar of English. It is not possible, for example, to learn about the change in question formation from Shakespeare's day to our own, evidenced in questions like:

> *Know'st thou this varlet?*

and

> *Do you know this varlet?*

without using notions such as verb, auxiliary, subject, pronoun, person, singular, plural, subject-auxiliary inversion, and so on.

My knowledge of secondary English departments in the Manchester area suggests that teachers are now paying much more attention to specifically linguistic features than they used to, and that they and their pupils are enjoying it. (The rapidly-increasing entry figures for the JMB's A-level English language paper show how much demand there is for a broad-based language course; the chief examiner's report on the scripts makes plain that many candidates handle technical terminology with assurance.) It would be tragic if a too-early revision to this innovative aspect of the English curriculum re-introduced the kind of grammatical work that was widespread in the 1950s; it was this unappealing and unproductive work which caused such a violent anti-language backlash among many English teachers - a backlash which is only just beginning to be overcome.

I am sure that there are ways in which the original Order can be improved but I think some of the suggestions in *The Case for Revising the Order* risk damaging just those aspects that are widely regarded as its strengths. It is also worth making the point that it is extremely difficult to formulate statements of attainment within a ten-level framework that will be applicable to all state schools in the country, that will not lead to undesirable teaching or assessment practices, and that will not give undue emphasis to those strands of English performance that are readily identifiable.

Professor Perera's letter admirably reflects the thinking of my 1989 National Curriculum English Working Group. A few of her remarks about spoken Standard English had some influence on the revised curriculum, but unfortunately other statements about Standard English remained unchanged, and the result was a muddle. In other respects Professor Perera's advice went unheeded. I am pleased to publish a major section of this letter, because after autumn 1995 there is some hope that the issues she raises can be reconsidered as teachers try to reformulate best practice in the new, more permissive climate of the 1995 English curriculum.

Revised English for Little England

The 1993 English Curriculum

After John Patten's acceptance on 9 September 1992 of NCC advice to review English in the National Curriculum, NCC moved quickly to begin a complete rewrite. In the *TES* of 18 September the Chairman, David Pascall, was reported as being adamant that there was no hidden agenda. He said: '*We are in no way influenced by the Centre for Policy Studies or indeed any other lobby group.*' Chris Woodhead, the NCC Chief Executive, said that the Council would be seeking a full range of opinions in carrying out its review. Attempts were made in press releases to suggest to the public and to teachers that the rewrite would build on the strengths of the Cox curriculum, and that alterations would be confined to the problems already discovered through the Warwick research.

These statements hid a conflict between the professional officers at NCC and the hidden agenda of the right-wing members of NCC, who were determined to rectify what they considered to be the 'progressive' values of the Cox curriculum. The criticisms of the Cox curriculum in Mr Patten's letter of 9 September (quoted on pp. 55–6) were much stronger than those in the NCC July document: *The Case for Revising the Order.* The Curriculum Council for Wales (CCW) had advised that in its judgment the balance of advantage was *against* a review of the Orders at the current time, but this advice was set aside by Mr Patten, and received little publicity. Mr Patten's agenda immediately became the brief for confidential meetings of NCC's English Review Group. At this time many people in education were enraged by the secrecy of this process, and by strong rumours that the aim of some NCC members was to destroy the Cox curriculum as soon as possible. The pronouncements of Lord Griffiths, as I have explained, indicated that powerful operators behind the scenes wanted a complete rewrite. Journalists, of course, were anxious to know what was going on, and the proceedings of NCC were inevitably regularly leaked.

The first English Review Group meeting took place on 12 October 1992 at the BP offices in London where David Pascall worked. This meeting agreed, according to the Minutes:

◆ revision will need to ensure that the Order requires a balanced approach to the teaching of reading, which gives greater prominence to phonics and the use of Reading Schemes;
◆ *Speaking and Listening:* it was agreed that the definition of Standard English as 'grammatically correct English spoken in any accent' was a reasonable working basis for the Review Team's work but further thought needed to be given to a precise definition.
◆ *Media Education:* it was felt that there should not be a distinct media strand in the new Order and that references to media texts should be related to opportunities for language development and comprehension;
◆ *Knowledge about Language:* the general view was that, as the requirements for grammar and spelling would be clearly defined at Key Stages 1 and 2, with appropriate progression in Key Stages 3 and 4, there was no need for a separate KAL strand. (Mrs Joan Clanchy, a member of NCC, later wrote in the *TES* of 5 March 1993 that at NCC Council discussions NCC dismissed knowledge about language as largely unnecessary in the drive back to basics. She wrote: *'Knowledge about Language' got hacked out of the Orders after 10 minutes' debate, and we got on to the fun of discussing whether the hymns of Charles Wesley should be added to the Key Stage 3 reading list.'*)
◆ *Information Technology:* given that information technology is adequately covered in AT5 in Technology, it was felt that there was no need for its inclusion in English.

When the NCC Council met on 20 October it was faced with a document that said the Secretary of State accepted Council's argument about the current Orders. This was followed by the four strong criticisms of the Cox Report in Mr Patten's letter. In other words, NCC had been moved willy-nilly from the carefully written July document to a complete acceptance that the Cox curriculum was in major respects inadequate.

The subsequent comments in the document for 20 October said that it would be necessary for the Review Team '*to define and place more emphasis on the basic skills of handwriting, spelling and grammar in the Programmes of Study and Statements of Attainment in Key Stages 1 and 2.*' On Standard English it was said that Professor Cox's Working Group 'bowed to those linguists who blanched at "correctness" ' and that the Council would insist that all children should conform to 'grammatically correct English spoken in any accent'. It was suggested that it was inappropriate to include Drama in an Order for English; it was argued that the National Curriculum should promote through the study of great art 'an understanding of our culture'. The reference to 'our culture' without any indication that this was problematic already gave a sign that NCC recommendations would place little emphasis on study of texts in English from other cultures.

The meetings on 12 and 20 October took place only a few weeks after the receipt of the Secretary of State's letter. It is clear from these meetings that many members of NCC were determined to rewrite the English curriculum as quickly as possible, and, as on later occasions, consultation with teachers would have little impact. Officials at NCC to whom I have talked agree that a decision to fight for a complete rewrite of the English curriculum (and History) had been agreed by the right-wing members at least a year before.

Leaks continued. Before Christmas 1992 the newspapers were full of arguments about a leaked list of authors to be enshrined in the National Curriculum. At this time I became very worried about the secrecy and lack of public debate about matters so vital for our children. I feared that the new curriculum would be published with careful manipulation of the media to ensure good publicity for what would be called a 'back to basics' campaign. Many officials at NCC and SEAC shared my concern. The joke in early 1993 was that we were all receiving nondescript brown paper envelopes which contained the latest horrendous proposals from NCC.

In February I received such a package with a full draft of the NCC proposals and I showed these to Judith Judd, education correspondent of the *Independent*. I believe that decisions about schooling deserve maximum coverage, and that government agencies must not be allowed to manipulate the media to give a false impression. I hoped that if the proposals came out in the *Independent*, at least there would be proper discussion of the issues. The danger of an NCC press conference followed by inaccurate headlines was that these would become the agenda for the debate, and that by the time teachers had prepared a rational response the story would have gone dead, and there would be little coverage. The leaked publication of the final draft led to an immediate debate about many issues, particularly the introduction of spoken Standard English to children from the age of five. Teachers were able to marshal their arguments against the new proposals, and to consider over a period of time how to show the general public that this new curriculum would be harmful to educational standards.

The authoritative rewrite was sent by David Pascall to Mr Patten on 5 March 1993, and published in April. My Working Group, which had brought together teachers of high quality, researchers with the highest international reputations in their subjects and an excellent Civil Service team, had laboured very hard to finish its recommendations in just over one year. NCC had taken no more than six months. It is not surprising that the NCC document, as well as reflecting unwelcome prejudice, also included many absurdities. What a waste of public money!

The NCC document concluded with a list of the names of organisations and individuals who had been consulted. Several people were angry to find their names included even though their advice had been almost entirely ignored. Names on the list who later protested at the mistakes and inadequacies in the document included David Allen, Henrietta Dombey, Katharine Perera, Margaret Meek Spencer and Ronald Carter. The impression was given that a major consultation exercise had taken place; in fact, crucial decisions on the new framework had been made before the consultation process began.

Resignation of Mrs Joan Clanchy

Behind the scenes a few members of NCC were most unhappy about the new curriculum. On 8 February 1993 Mrs Joan Clanchy, a member of the NCC Council and headmistress of North London Collegiate School, 'resigned in despair'. The North London Collegiate School is an independent school with an excellent academic reputation. In her resignation letter to John Patten, Mrs Clanchy warned him:

❛ the dominant aim has become a curriculum designed for tests and the result is a model of English teaching which is barren and anti-intellectual. Your predecessors did a great deal of work, through the Commission under Professor Sir John Kingman and the working party under Professor Brian Cox, to reinforce lively, sensible teaching which would enhance love of literature in this country. (*TES*, 5 March 1993).

In contrast, she believed the new curriculum would lower standards. She strongly supported the view that children should learn to speak Standard English and to write grammatically, but she condemned the new English Order for being written in short phrases which 'spray instructions like machine-gun fire'. She told the *TES*: '*I am alarmed to think the National Curriculum, in its rolling review, is going to adopt this confrontational style of giving orders to teachers.*' She was also sharply critical of the consultation process, and accused the Council of ignoring expert advice in favour of the views of right-wingers. In the *TES* of 5 March 1993 she wrote in an essay headed 'Terse but not to the point':

It is well known that some members of the Council belong to right-wing think tanks. I have never objected to that because, of course, such organisations are going to produce activists who will have ideas to contribute. But I did object as a Council member to only being given Centre for Policy Studies pamphlets to read by way of homework.

She revealed that right-wingers such as Professor O'Hear and Dr Marks were invited to address the NCC Council without a counter-view being aired:

At my first Council meeting, Professor Anthony O'Hear addressed us on his view of the allegedly pernicious influence of Dewey on primary education. In no sense was it a debate because there was no representative from any teacher-training institution to reply or give a view on the current interpretations of Dewey's work. This year we were sent copies of Dr John Marks's 'Value for Money in Education' and he addressed us on it, again without a counter view being aired. We were sent Stuart Deuchar's pamphlet on history in the Campaign for Real Education series, but not Chris Husband's rebuttal of it. We were not sent copies of Professor Eric Bolton's and Professor Paul Black's pamphlets on 'Putting the record straight'.

Mrs Clanchy concluded that a quango of 'plain' men and women with a team of three professional officers whose advice was often ignored was not the right body to rewrite the work of Kingman and Cox. In a letter of 21 April 1993 in the *Independent*, Mrs Clanchy praised the treatment of grammar in the Cox curriculum, and said about the revised curriculum: '*the new one has been constructed for tests as if the Highway Code had been narrowed down to instructions on the three-point turn.*' Mrs Clanchy's courageous resignation and public stance had great influence on the subsequent debate. In my articles, lectures and radio and television interviews at that time I insisted that good teachers in independent schools would not conform to the new curriculum, and so they would gain a considerable advantage over state schools, which would be forced to obey the prescriptions of this new sterile curriculum. Mrs Clanchy's resignation brought the opposition of independent schools into the public domain.

The main objection to the April 1993 English curriculum was that it was too prescriptive, and would lower standards because originality and enthusiasm would be stifled. When I met David Pascall at the Shakespeare conference in 1992 I tried unsuccessfully to persuade him that to impose a curriculum on English teachers which they believed to be misconceived was a sure recipe for disaster. Teachers must believe in what they are doing; the great success of the Cox curriculum was that teachers felt a sense of ownership, that although its demands were rigorous, and some, as with knowledge about language, innovative, it reflected good practice. The new curriculum was largely driven by the narrow demands of what could be easily assessed in paper-and-pencil tests. It was restrictive, not enabling.

For example, at level 1 (age 5) the document said pupils '*should be taught to distinguish between the essential and less important when speaking*'. This is an hilarious example of ignorance about the social relations between a teacher and a five-year-old. When children of five talk about the sweets and ice-cream and clothes they wore to the theatre, should the teacher tell them these matters are less important than the play? How absurd! This kind of prescription shows a desire for authority with no sense of the real learning experiences of little children, who need maximum encouragement to speak and express their own interests.

The Welsh perspective

When the Right took over crucial positions of power on NCC and SEAC they forgot to do the same for the Curriculum Council for Wales (CCW). Richard Daugherty, its Chair, was supported by teachers sympathetic to the Cox curriculum. On 9 March 1993 the CCW submitted to Mr David Hunt, Secretary of State for Wales, a revised curriculum different in crucial respects from the one devised by the NCC at York, and in the view of teachers vastly superior. Behind the scenes attempts were made by Mr Patten and his supporters to play down the importance of this division, and even to prevent the publication of the Welsh document, but fortunately this did not happen. I discovered from a former student of mine, then a member of the CCW, what was going on, and alerted the press, who knew a good story when they saw one. There was considerable publicity, particularly in the *Observer*. Would Wales be allowed to go its own way, or would Wales be forced to kow-tow to the requirements of the English NCC at York?

Richard Daugherty's letter to David Hunt of 9 March 1993 listed three ways in which the Welsh proposals differed from those submitted by NCC to ministers in England:

❧ 1. We believe it is not appropriate to introduce a requirement to use Standard English in speaking and listening before level 5; increasing competence in standard spoken English is thus a feature of our proposals from key stage 2 onwards.

2. We are also recommending that the reading required of pupils should be set out in terms of criteria and categories rather than as lists of authors/texts. This consistent framework across all four key stages will, in our view, ensure that pupils read a wide range of suitable fiction and non-fiction texts. In this respect, as with the recommendations on Standard English, we believe our proposals are more appropriate for pupils learning English in Wales.

3. There are several other respects in which it is desirable for the revised Order to reinforce the strengths of the current Order.

The Welsh document made it abundantly clear, as the NCC document did not, that the consultation process revealed no desire among teachers for radical change. In this respect the NCC document was deliberately misleading. Mrs Joan Clanchy wrote in the *TES* on 23 April 1993 about the differences between the York and the Welsh reports: '*in their introductions to their reports they interpret the consultation process differently. Both had received the same 173 responses. York reports them as showing 'little consensus', Cardiff noted considerable agreement on some points: notably, support for the current Order and concern that English teaching should not be driven by assessment.*' Section 3.3. of the Welsh document reads:

❧ There was broad agreement among respondents in Wales on the following aspects of the review:
   ◆   support for the current Order;
   ◆   agreement that the integration of Spelling and Handwriting was desirable;

- support for the equal weighting of the three attainment targets;
- concern that the model of English teaching should not be assessment driven;
- recognition of the need for a balanced approach to the teaching of early reading;
- support for the clarification of more advanced reading skills;
- agreement that non-statutory guidance was the most appropriate means of indicating the range of reading desirable in each key stage;
- concern regarding the understanding and interpretation of the term 'our literary heritage';
- concern that standard English should be regarded as a form of language appropriate in certain contexts for speaking and writing and that confidence and fluency in speech are not peculiar to standard English.

In its amplification of Richard Daugherty's third statement, that there was need to build on the strengths of the current Order, the Welsh document specified two particular concerns (4.1. and 4.2. in appendix 1):

❝ 4.1. The apparent departure from the underpinning rationale of the current Order which drew extensively on the Bullock and Kingman Reports, the implementation of GCSE and the work of the National Writing and Oracy Projects.
4.2. The implicit narrowing of the range of learning experiences which would encourage the perception that the revised English curriculum is more mechanistic and restrictive than that exemplified in the current Order.

This is urbane Civil Service language. Translated into my words this means:

- the NCC in England has rejected the ideas of all the major studies of the last 21 years concerning good practice in the teaching of English;
- the NCC curriculum is narrow, mechanistic and restrictive.

The publicity given to this Welsh document was a great encouragement as teachers tried to publicise the professional consensus that the new NCC curriculum would lower standards.

NCC opposition to good practice

The NCC curriculum was not without some virtues. There were useful organisational and presentational changes. The document was easier to grasp because Programmes of Study and Statements of Attainment were laid out side by side, and because each attainment target was subdivided into strands. Many teachers welcomed the decision to combine all the components of Writing into one attainment target. Almost everyone agreed, however, that such changes could have been introduced into the existing Orders without a complete rewrite.

There were seven areas in particular where the new NCC curriculum offended against good practice: the mechanistic treatment of grammar; the narrowness of the prescriptions about reading; the introduction of spoken Standard English at too early an age; the almost complete removal of knowledge about language; the prescribed reading lists; the reduced emphasis on media studies; and the tokenism in references to English in other cultures.

Grammar, punctuation, writing

English was treated almost like a foreign language, with teachers required to drill six-year-olds in mechanical exercises. In Writing there was insufficient emphasis on imagination and the need to write to communicate meanings to real audiences.

In a brilliant, witty article on 7 May 1993 in *Education*, Graham Frater (previously Chief HMI for English and an adviser for my National Curriculum English Working Group) wrote about how in the search for precision the emphasis shifted towards 'measuring the measurable because of its measurability'. And so for Writing the NCC defined five strands (Forms of Writing; Grammar; Punctuation; Spelling; Handwriting) against one for composition. At level 2 for Punctuation we have: '*in a sequence of simple sentences, use full stops and capital letters correctly in at least 50 per cent of instances.*' Frater said that in practice such explicitness is apt to deliver arbitrary assessments, and he continued by quoting the poet Roy Campbell:

> '*They use the snaffle and the curb all right,*
> *But where's the bloody horse?*'

When the authors of the levels of attainment try to introduce ideas of quality they show their inexperience and incompetence. Words like 'complex', 'coherently', 'interesting' and 'original' are linked to specific levels with no sense of how impossible it is to define these words with any degree of clarity. The critics of the Cox curriculum had called it 'woolly', but the NCC efforts had produced a mishmash even less precise. Frater quoted examples of three levels of attainment for Writing, and challenged the reader to work out whether they are in ascending or descending order. His examples from the NCC document read:

◆ Convey ideas and themes convincingly through the effective use of vocabulary;
◆ Express meaning clearly and effectively, using a wide vocabulary;
◆ Produce sustained and well-organised writing in which the meaning is both clear and interesting.

Frater commented: *'in fact, level 6 comes first and they are in descending order. If you were wrong, you probably are or have been a teacher; if right, you must be David Pascall.'*

The teaching of reading

In the attainment target for 'Reading' there was insufficient emphasis on reading for enjoyment, and on the need to understand what is read and to respond with enthusiasm. In an essay 'Some thoughts on the proposals for Reading' in *Language Matters* (1992-3, *3*, pp. 15-16) Henrietta Dombey, Principal Lecturer in Primary Language and Literacy at the University of Brighton, commented that not everything was bad in the new curriculum. The gentler and more informed voices of the professional officers broke through in recommendations that at level 1 pupils should *'experience stories and literature which include patterned language'* and *'act out stories they have had read to them'*. But these occasional gentle moments are wiped out in the memory by strident and highly questionable prescriptions such as the opening sentence of the Programmes of Study for Key Stage 1: *'Pupils learn to read when they are taught the necessary skills of which phonics is an essential component.'* The ABC had become a totem, set up as the very first Statement of Attainment at level 1, 'taking us back to the chanting classrooms of the nineteenth century', and from level 1 we lose the recognition that print carries meaning. At level 2 children should *'identify two-letter consonant blends and the most common digraphs'*. Henrietta Dombey asks:

To what end? This building block conception encourages carrying the teaching of phonics beyond the point for which there is any clear justification from reputable research. While there is some reference to other cues (phonic, graphic, syntactic and contextual, but not picture clues), the orchestration of these into a smooth harmonious process receives no mention.

Such criticism from professionals was appearing in great numbers in journals, such as *Language Matters* and the *TES*, but few politicians seemed aware of the chorus of disapproval (there were some notable courageous exceptions among Conservative MPs, for example Sir Malcolm Thornton and Alan Howarth). In the *TES* of 30 April 1993 Bill Laar, Chief Inspector for the City of Westminster, wrote:

The section on comprehension is particularly weak, moving from what is in fact a word recognition exercise at Level 1, through bland ambiguities at Levels 2 and 3, until inference and deduction are finally reached at Level 4 with an unremarkable example: 'use evidence in a text to infer a meaning or an attitude and draw together a number of clues to grasp a factual point the author is making.' This seems to suggest that children who have mastered the most complex of reading challenges - the initial stages - cannot cope with the so-called 'higher order' reading skills until then, nor even have encountered them.

In an article 'Moulded Minds', in the *TES* of 18 June 1993, Shona Walton, Chair of NATE, described the horror of primary school teachers at a conference when they were confronted with the revised curriculum. The new proposals on reading, she said, betray a total ignorance, or a wilful dismissal, of the research of thirty years:

Teachers at my briefings gasped at the requirements to identify final sounds of words at Level 1 and were alarmed by the undervaluing of developing enjoyment, interest and meaning-making. The new proposals focus almost entirely on a narrow conception of word identification and on children spotting 'correct' meanings in texts, rather than bringing their own understandings.

Shona Walton described the new curriculum as 'anti-intellectual': *'it is not designed to teach children how to think, or to make their own meanings, but emphasises through the assessment framework, the ability to conform to conventional correctness, and to produce prescribed responses.'*

In the *TES* of 7 May 1993 a major article appeared, 'A Love of Nostalgia', written by three well-known professionals: Myra Barrs, Director of the Centre for Language in Primary Education, Henrietta Dombey and Graham Frater. They concluded:

> The new English National Curriculum, especially that part of it to be assessed, would (if it were implemented and tested on from 1995) be one that ignored most of what has been discovered about the development and teaching of oral and written language over the past 30 years. It would be based on an unreal vision of what children are like and how best they can be taught. It would be imposed on the experts on the ground against a strong consensus of professional advice.

A letter from two teachers in the *Independent* of 5 February 1993 brought out why so many good teachers to whom I spoke in 1993 were so desperately worried:

> There are teachers who will welcome the proposals.... Teachers who want an undemanding job, giving pupils regular doses of copying from punctuation books, will support the proposals. They will be able to sit ticking neat sentences or reading the paper in front of a silent class.... Schools that have had difficulties recruiting specialist English teachers will be able to give a 'bit of English' to any teacher with a spare lesson on the time table because they can fill the time by practising exams questions from the SATs.

Such lazy teachers might be in a minority, but the decision to revise the curriculum, as we have seen, led many teachers to abandon innovation.

Spoken Standard English

For Key Stage 1 the NCC proposed:

> Pupils should be introduced with appropriate sensitivity to the basic conventions of Standard English.... The key features of Standard English grammar in this key stage are subject-verb agreement, effective word order and correct and consistent use of verb tenses.

This meant that by the age of seven children would be expected to speak Standard English, and if they spoke dialect at home to have changed their language use. To achieve this teachers would have to start correcting their pupils' speech from the day they arrived at school. Fierce criticisms of this proposal were vigorously opposed by David Pascall who, because he had no experience of teaching children in the classroom, simply and dogmatically thought he could start a successful campaign to get rid of sloppy speech among the nation's children. He committed himself to the view that all children from the age of five should be made to speak what he called 'grammatically correct' spoken Standard English, even in the playground. When a clever journalist asked him what 'grammatically correct' meant, he replied: 'They shouldn't split the infinitive.' A popular joke at the time, repeated at many conferences for teachers, was that in future children who wished to split the infinitive would have to go behind the bicycle shed.

In the statements of attainment for 'Speaking and Listening', many of the statements were written in a punitive, negative tone, with a focus on possible errors that must be avoided in order to achieve the statement. In general, there was a focus on forms rather than meaning or purpose, and there was an apparently arbitrary selection and ordering of structures that were to be either used or shunned.

I later challenged David Pascall in the *Independent on Sunday* (2 May 1993) on these matters, pointing out that it would be impossible to assess children's use of what he called grammatically correct spoken Standard English without tape-recording, since it is not possible to perform a grammatical analysis while attending to what someone is saying. For example, at level 5 pupils are supposed to make use of demonstratives, reflexive pronouns, adjectives, adverbs, connectives and prepositions. They will probably use all of these in even a short piece of talk (except, perhaps, reflexive pronouns), but it would be absurd for a teacher to have to tick them off in some way. Tape-recording of each child would have to last 20 to 30 minutes, and would have to be followed by transcription so the examiner could check carefully for grammatical errors. The whole process could take weeks for one class, and is clearly impossible. David Pascall replied to me in a letter in the *Independent on Sunday* the following week (9 May) saying that he could not see why I was so bothered about assessment. By May 1993 it was becoming clear that assessment would be reduced to paper-and-pencil tests, and that Speaking and Listening would probably not be examined. The result, of course, is that these activities would be downgraded, for teachers would be forced to concentrate on what *was* to be tested.

Professor Gillian Brown of Cambridge University published an important letter in the *Independent* (20 April 1993). Professor Brown, a member of the Kingman Committee, was largely responsible for the model of language in the Kingman Report. In her letter she insisted that all children should be taught Standard English because it is a lingua franca used throughout the world. '*However*,' she writes, '*it is worrying that the new curriculum requires the teaching of spoken Standard English to begin at age five.'*

❧ Those who framed it cannot have appreciated that the only stable model of a standard language is to be found in its written form. About 15% of the population speak Standard English and even they frequently produce non-standard spoken forms.

How on earth is an East Anglian five-year-old who hears a mishmash of dialects on television, and parents, relatives, schoolfriends, postmen, bus drivers, and shopkeepers using the dialectical paradigm 'I was, you was, he was, we was, they was' supposed to distinguish between the bits that are all right and the bits that won't do?

She continued with words central to professional opinion on the teaching of spoken Standard English:

❧ Only after the child can read and write confidently, at least at reading age eight, is it reasonable to begin working from the relatively stable forms of the written language to point out grammatical differences between the standard language and the dialect.

As a member of the Kingman Committee, I was impressed by the admirable intelligence and common sense of Professor Gillian Brown, just as later I was impressed by similar qualities in Professor Katharine Perera, the linguist on my National Curriculum English Working Group whose letter I quoted at the end of my previous chapter. NCC's failure to enlist this kind of professional expertise on its committees and working groups meant that its recommendations for classroom teaching were out of touch with research and good practice, and its definitions of Standard English often inaccurate. In an essay in *Language Matters* (1992-3, *3*, pp. 9-10) Katharine Perera objected that the NCC requirements revealed an inadequate understanding of the differences between prepared and spontaneous speech, and between speech and writing:

❧ Good oral communication is intelligible, understandable, appropriate to the situation, and effective in achieving its purpose. Standard English can be all of those things but it is not necessarily so just by virtue of being standard: non-standard speech is often completely understandable and, in the right circumstances, both appropriate and effective, while Standard English (like any other variety) can be ineffective if the speaker is vague or pompous, verbose or platitudinous.

The statements of attainment gave undue importance to the forms of language and insufficient weight to effective communication. Katharine

Perera also stressed that the way people speak says something about the social group with which they identify, and to which they are loyal:

❝ Pupils may, unconsciously, value more highly the sense of solidarity with family and friends that comes from saying 'We haven't seen nobody' than the perhaps dubious prestige of 'We haven't seen anybody'. If they are to add the forms of Standard English to their linguistic repertoire, they need to see the point of it....

What was so infuriating about the situation from 1992 to 1993 is that wise advice of this kind, from people with experience in research and teaching in the classroom, was so easily available and so wantonly put aside by David Pascall and NCC.

The letter in the *Independent* (20 April 1993) after Gillian Brown's was written by Pat and Clive Wolfe. It began: '*What the mandarins of Government have failed to recognise by enforcing teachers of English to feed "standard" or "correct" grammar and vocabulary to schoolchildren is that in doing so they are implying that the child's parents, relations and peers are at best ignoramuses, at worst fools.*' The tests would constitute a judgment on class background, and working-class children would fail. The confidence of little children would be undermined by having their speech, which is perfectly comprehensible, altered in an apparently arbitrary way. Every class teacher knows that the problem with many children aged five is to build up confidence so that they are not afraid to address the whole class. David Pascall's prescriptions ignored real childen and real classroom situations.

Knowledge about Language

The new curriculum almost entirely removed the broad study of language advocated in the Cox curriculum. I have already explained why this was so harmful. As soon as it was announced that the curriculum would be revised, many teachers stopped bothering about the Cox requirements with regard to knowledge about language. Why work hard on elements in the curriculum soon to be eliminated? Teachers had taught grammar with enthusiasm in the context of interesting activities which consider language as a whole (its history, regional variations, social contexts, changes in vocabulary and grammar which are part of the living language). The new curriculum reduced sensitivity to language to a series of mechanical exercises.

Prescribed authors and texts

The NCC book lists leaked to the press in December 1992 provoked outrage among specialists on children's reading. For primary school children they concentrated almost entirely on traditional classics. Sally Feldman, editor of *Treasure Island,* the children's book series on Radio 4, called these lists 'a betrayal of children, of their literature, and of the experience of reading' (*The Times,* 1 January 1993). She admired Lewis Carroll, Kenneth Grahame, E. Nesbit and A.A. Milne, of course, but why, she asked, have our best contemporary writers been ignored in favour of 'this outmoded spectre of childhood, frozen in a sentimental, ultra-traditional frame?'

❛ Seemingly unwilling to contemplate any comparisons between cherished classics and new works, the compilers of these lists have erected once more a barrier between the books that are good for you and the others. This attitude can cause irreparable damage.
The culture offered to our children is dominated by the values of the British Empire in its heyday. The books are mostly written from the point of view of the English upper middle classes for their children. When the list does venture away from this model it makes some extraordinary clumsy leaps. Why choose *Huckleberry Finn,* a book that is defiantly impenetrable even to the most lettered adult? There are plenty of modern books that mean far more to children - Gene Kemp's irrepressible *Turbulent Term of Tyke Tyler* (Puffin) or James Berry's spirited retelling of the *Anancy Spiderman* stories.

Sally Feldman listed many other recent children's books which are not on the list but are wonderfully successful in persuading children to enjoy reading. She recommended a child who is enchanted by *Alice's Adventures in Wonderland* to try *The Mouse and His Child* by Russell Hoban. Why include Richmal Crompton's *William* and not Sue Townsend's *Adrian Mole* or Helen Cresswell's gloriously eccentric *Bagthorpes?* Children are fascinated by problems of their own times, and should read compelling books about apartheid such as Beverley Naidoo's *Chains of Fire.* Seven- to eleven-year-olds might read *Carrie's War* by Nina Bawden, an excellent account of the experience of evacuation. And so on.

In the *Sunday Telegraph* on 5 October 1992 John Marenbon said only time can give a book classic status, which is true enough, but then went on to say that prescribed lists should not include anything written during the last twenty or thirty years. Such prescription inevitably weakens a teacher's power to help children to enjoy reading.

Sally Feldman also attacked the omissions in the list of poetry. Masefield, Donne, Yeats and Larkin make it, but no women do, nor any black writer. There is no mention of modern poets such as Michael Rosen, Roger McGough, John Agard or Brian Patten, who have done so much to make poetry available for today's children. She recommended eclectic collections like Michael Rosen's *Kingfisher Collection of Children's Poetry* and Brian Patten's *Puffin Book of 20th Century Children's Poetry* in which modern poets and songwriters sit alongside those who have been hallowed by the National Curriculum Council seal of approval. The NCC list, she said, would 'introduce a two tier system - the ones who can manage *Treasure Island* and *Oliver Twist*, and the failures'.

When the April 1993 NCC curriculum was finally published, concessions had been made because of these criticisms, and the lists included some authors mentioned by Sally Feldman, plus some women and non-white authors. But these early lists reveal the state of mind of NCC members. In the *TES* of 15 January 1993 Bill Laar echoed the view of Sally Feldman that the lists were of works of another age, and that they shun issues that concern the contemporary world and its children: '*They largely ignore revolutionary social and industrial changes, the extraordinary developments in communication which have shaped and continue to transform our lives.*' The NCC group who took over the English curriculum was deeply afraid of modern society, trapped in fantasies of a lost golden age of Victorian childhood, and desperate to prevent young children today from being subjected to the realities of the modern world.

Although in April 1993 the lists were much improved (presumably because of the influence of NCC's professional officers), there were still major objections. There were oddities. Solzhenitsyn suddenly appeared in a list of authors who all wrote originally in English, and Ibsen in a list of dramatists. No other authors from the continent of Europe were listed. Ted Hughes was included in the lists for Key Stage 3 but not for Key Stage 4, while Seamus Heaney and R. S. Thomas appeared in both. Robert Bridges was included for Key Stage 4 but not Thomas Hardy. In Key Stage 4, why Abse and not Causley? Tony Harrison was excluded presumably because he writes verse attacking the Government. In my opinion he is the most exciting English poet writing today, and I know that teachers have found that young people often react positively and with genuine enthusiasm to poems such as his *V*, which deals with skinheads in Leeds.

These lists were greeted with abuse and mockery. The funniest attack on the NCC list, 'John Patten's tarnished treasury of English dirge', was written by the poet James Fenton in the *Independent* (19 April 1993). He particularly attacked the list called 'Classic Poetry' for Key Stage 2. These examples were recommended reading for seven- to eleven-year-olds: John Masefield (*Sea Fever*), W.H. Longfellow (*The Wreck of the Hesperus*), Edward Lear (*The Jumblies*), Walter de la Mare (*The Listeners*), Lewis Carroll (*You Are Old, Father William*), T.S. Eliot (*Macavity, the Mystery Cat*), Alfred Noyes (*The Highwayman*), Eleanor Farjeon (*It was Long Ago*) and Hilaire Belloc (*Tarantella*). There are other poems under a heading called 'Verse', but these 'Classic' poems were intended to introduce children to the notion of high art in verse. James Fenton commented on this choice:

❧ And look at it! Look at the fatheadedness of it, the unambitiousness of it, the this-is-what-I-was-brought-up-on-ness of it (and therefore this is what I expect to be inflicted on my children, is the implication). It is not borne of any thought for what is classic in poetry. I should suspect rather that it is borne of a hatred for poetry, which says to itself, 'Thus far and no further I am prepared to read.'

The Wreck, Fenton says, is not even good Longfellow, and Alfred Noyes is not a 'Classic' poet. Fenton enjoyed himself by pointing out that *The Highwayman* and *The Wreck of the Hesperus* both describe a girl being tied up and killed: '*In other words, someone on the National Curriculum Council is keen on tying up, torturing and killing little girls. I think whoever it is should be exposed.*' Fenton was leg-pulling, of course, but if lady members of NCC had known more about cultural analysis they might have been aware that Victorian and Edwardian literature often depicts women as submissive and dominated by men. Fenton ended on a more serious note by recommending two poems which are real 'classics' and should be on the list: Shakespeare's *When Icicles Hang by the Wall* and Blake's *The Tyger*.

Media studies

Media Studies had been reduced to newspapers, with film and television excluded, presumably under the influence of the kind of arguments Dr Marks put forward in his lecture to the Institute of Economic Affairs and John Major's fear that children will watch *Neighbours* instead of reading Shakespeare. The British Film Institute was so incensed by this exclusion that in association with the *TES* it organised a special Commission of Inquiry into English which took place in the National Film Theatre on 26 and 27 November 1993. This was chaired by Baroness Warnock. The

Commissioners were Professor Robin Alexander, Professor of Primary Education at the University of Leeds; Professor Marilyn Butler, who was at that time King Edward VII Professor of English Literature, King's College, Cambridge, and had just been appointed Rector of Exeter College, Oxford; Alan Howarth, Conservative MP for Stratford-upon-Avon since 1983 and a Junior Minister in the Department of Education and Science between 1989 and 1992; and Anthony Smith, President of Magdalen College, Oxford, who has written a number of books on the media. Witnesses included Colin MacCabe from the British Film Institute, Professor Roger Scruton of Boston University, Margaret Maden, County Education Officer for Warwickshire, Lady Howe, Chair of the Broadcasting Standards Council, and many other well-known teachers. I took part as a witness in a session called 'Cultural Heritage and Cultural Analysis: What is English for?', but I must admit that after a year of campaigning in newspapers and on radio and television I had nothing new to say. The arguments about the media I shall consider in chapters 9 and 10. What is interesting about the Commissioners' conclusions from such a high-powered group is that they found there was a considerable degree of consensus among the participants. In their conclusions they said:

> ... our predominant concern is with the confrontational nature of public debate about education in Britain. It is characterised by simplistic dichotomies: 'traditional' versus 'progressive'; 'phonics' versus 'look and say'; 'Shakespeare' versus 'soap opera'. But despite the wide range of values expressed by witnesses we heard, we found no evidence of entrenched opposition or irreconcilable polarities; there was, in fact, a large measure of agreement. In our view it is a caricature to portray education as dominated by sectarianism.

The Cox Report reflected this large measure of agreement. The Commissioners' conclusions draw attention to the level of fantasy among right-wingers who accuse teachers of extreme distaste for spelling or Shakespeare or phonics. During the debates about the curriculum in 1993 the newspaper coverage was often hostile to teachers, and misrepresentation of their views was common.

Writers from other cultures

In an essay in *Language Matters* (1992-3, no.3,) Sibani Raychaudhuri, Inspector for Bilingualism in the London Borough of Tower Hamlets, pointed out that the NCC document gave very few examples of literature which reflects the cultural heritage of ethnic minority children. Also the document gave no weight to the important influence on English literature of works such as *The Arabian Nights*. Stories such as 'The Magic Carpet', 'The Jinni in the Bottle' and 'Sinbad the Sailor' are memorable events in children's lives. Also in this issue of *Language Matters*, Michael Rosen, a highly successful writer for children, pointed out that to separate out 'classic poetry' and 'established children's fiction' from 'texts from a variety of traditions' tends to marginalise non-white writers as 'other'. He said that during a debate at the Booksellers' Association annual conference in 1993 David Pascall actually used the word 'other' in this context. The distrust of non-white writers runs deep in the decision to revise the English curriculum. Rosen wrote:

> When we see that *The Jungle Book* is 'established' even though at least one of the stories in the book 'Her Majesty's Servants' is explicitly racist about Afghans and supremacist about British rule in India, then we are entitled to ask some serious questions. *What Katy Did* and *Peter Pan* are fanatic about ascribing roles to girls, the snobberies towards working-class people in *Just William*, *The Wind in the Willows* and *The Railway Children* are very unpleasant, and assumptions about native Americans in *The Little House on the Prairie* need careful negotiation.

Like many other commentators, Rosen pointed out the mistake in the reading lists where *A Child's Garden of Verses* is described as an 'anthology' which was edited by Robert Louis Stevenson, although in fact he wrote it all himself. Like Fenton, he was unhappy about the inclusion of *The Highwayman*, with its sacrificial female death.

All these criticisms show the folly of prescribed lists. Major areas are omitted. Teachers must be free to help children to enjoy literature by choosing appropriate books, and forcing so-called 'classics' down their throats is counter-productive. Rosen's criticism of the racism in the reading lists brought out why cultural analysis is so essential in the curriculum. Children enjoy reading Kipling and many other writers whose beliefs may be politically incorrect for the right-wing or the left-wing. Shakespeare is in many ways anti-democratic. As I argued when, in chapter 2, I was discussing Dr Marks's lecture, children need to understand that great works often subscribe to a system of values which today we may find unacceptable. As they proceed through secondary school they need to be encouraged to discuss these matters, and to be introduced to the conflicting opinions about aesthetic values which have engaged the attention of literary theorists from Plato and Aristotle to the present day.

In a letter in the *Guardian* (19 May 1993), eighteen authors whose names or works had been included in the NCC reading lists wrote to dissociate themselves from this exercise. Their objections were:

- the lists are authoritarian in that they come without either debate or commentary;
- they have a negative effect upon teachers' understanding of and enthusiasm for literature through delimiting and dictating choice;
- they are unrepresentative of many cultural traditions that have prevailed in the past and are important today.

As the authors trenchantly stated: '*if we are "approved" authors, then by implication other writers are "not approved". We do not wish to be part of such a blanket, uncritical rejection of fellow writers.*'

Responses from Higher Education

In November 1992, twenty-one university professors of English wrote to *The Times* to lambast the Government's plans to rewrite the English curriculum. On 11 June 1993 the letter was reprinted in the *Times Higher Education Supplement* with 576 signatories who were all university teachers of English, including 42 Oxbridge academics. The original letter was drafted by the left-wing Terry Eagleton, Warton Professor of English at Oxford, but the 576 signatures included many who were known to be traditional in their sympathies. I quote the letter in its entirety because it splendidly sums up the moral objections to the new curriculum, and illustrates the new danger that English studies in schools would be at odds in many respects with English studies in higher education:

As university teachers of English, we view with dismay the Government's proposed reforms to the teaching of English in schools. Like all academics, we expect sound grammar and spelling from our students; but the Government's doctrinaire preoccupation with these skills betrays a disastrously reductive, mechanistic understanding of English studies.
Similarly, its evident hostility to regional and working-class forms of speech in the classroom betrays a prejudice which has little or no intellectual basis, and which is seriously harmful to the well-being and self-esteem of many children.

We are all committed to the study of Shakespeare; but to make such study compulsory for 14 year olds, as the minister intends, is to risk permanently alienating a large number of children from the pleasurable understanding of classical literary works.

Even more disquieting is the plan for a dictatorially imposed canon of supposedly great works, in gross and wilful ignorance of more than two decades of intellectual debate among literary academics over questions of literary value and the literary canon.

These philistine, ill-informed proposals would strip English of much that we and many of our colleagues regard as most precious and educational about it. They threaten to reduce a living language to a dead one, and a vital literary heritage to a mummified relic.

They would do serious damage to the moral and social development of our children, and to the cultural life of society as a whole, and all who are concerned with such matters should oppose in the strongest terms.

A further blast from higher education fell upon NCC on 1 May 1993, when forty professors and lecturers of English published a letter in the *Independent*. This letter, quite brief, had been rejected by *The Times*. It attacked the new curriculum's '*unacceptable degree of political and statutory control over classroom teaching*', listed the major objections I have described in this chapter, and ended: '*a curriculum which so misrepresents the subject of English is an inadequate preparation for its study at higher levels.*'

The revised curriculum was sent out for consultation. Teachers sent in a spate of criticisms of the kind I have described. When the revisions of the revised curriculum were published in September, almost all this advice had been ignored, and most faults remained. This September document was not widely circulated, and many primary school teachers never saw a copy. By this time Sir Ron Dearing was in charge, and a new slimmed-down curriculum was promised for 1994.

6

Examinations and Boycotts

SEAC and secrecy

While in 1992 and 1993 right-wingers on NCC were busy rewriting the English curriculum, their associates on SEAC were busy preparing a series of old-fashioned tests which enraged the teaching profession. In 1989 after my English Working Group had submitted its Report I gave numerous talks to teachers to explain our rationale. I was given a sympathetic reception, but on almost every occasion teachers voiced their worries that all our good intentions could be ruined by inappropriate arrangements for assessment. They were proved right.

Already in 1990 teachers had encountered major problems with the pilot Standard Assessment Tasks (SATs) for Key Stage 1. The NUT independently investigated 2 per cent of primary schools, and published *Testing: Who Carries the Load?* which particularly stressed that the workload was too heavy. This led to improvements in 1991, though the SATs workload still remained far too great. The NUT also argued that continuous teacher assessment is the most effective form of assessment, and that short, timed tests could not hope to cover all aspects of the curriculum. The danger was that a 'mini-curriculum' would emerge, and that the SATs would bear little relation to the richness of the pilot schools' own plans for the curriculum. This major problem could only be answered by coursework, particularly for Key Stages 1 to 3; the Cox English curriculum was prepared on the understanding that coursework would provide a major input into the assessment process.

These problems did not make headline news, and primary school teachers were left to struggle on with little public concern for their plight. All this changed dramatically after Lord Brian Griffiths took over

SEAC in August 1991. His attempts to impose simple paper-and-pencil tests, particularly on Key Stage 3 English, provoked a furore of considerable political significance.

What happened behind the scenes was revealed by Peter Harding, the English teacher from Lincolnshire whom I mentioned in chapter 4. In an article on 15 January 1993 in the *TES* he explained how in September 1992 he was invited to serve for three years on the English committee of SEAC. The brief of the committee was '*to offer advice to Council on issues arising concerning examinations and examination syllabuses, to keep under review.... the development of assessment arangements in the relevant subject area, and to offer advice to Council on matters arising.*' The whole committee was to meet only three times a year, though ad hoc sub-committees of two or three members could be set up from time to time.

The whole committee met on 30 October 1992 under the new chair, Dr John Marenbon. The next meeting was scheduled for 4 March 1993. In between these two meetings the final pilots for Key Stage 3 English tests were being trialled. By the March meeting the trials would be completed, material for the summer printed, and some material sent to schools, all without the committee being involved. When Harding wrote to Marenbon to ask for an earlier meeting, particularly as English teachers were so critical of the pilot tests, Marenbon fobbed him off by saying that this could only happen if Council asked for advice. Marenbon, of course, was a member of Council, and, typically, power was kept at a distance from the teachers on the English committee. Earlier in 1992 Michael Jones, Chair of the National Association of Advisers in English (NAAE), had resigned from SEAC because of what he called the false reverence for pencil-and-paper tests, and because SEAC was determined to force teachers to comply with testing procedures which they believed were not in the interest of their pupils (*Independent*, 22 April 1993).

In his *TES* article Harding complained about the infrequency of the English committee's meetings, and about Marenbon's failure to understand the problems of English teachers. Harding wrote:

❦ ... the chairman of the English committee, who is also a member of Council, is the director of English studies at Trinity College, Cambridge, an expert in medieval philosophy - very remote from the experience of the average school pupil in the English state education system. He probably meets about 0.05 per cent of all A-level English students each year who achieve an interview in the ivory towers of Trinity! His views often differ from the majority of the English committee, and yet his is the voice heard at Council meetings: a voice whose views are clearly outlined in his Centre for Policy Studies pamphlet 'English Our English'...

Teachers who were members of SEAC's mathematics committee, chaired by Dr John Marks, similarly complained that their views were not heard by Council. Perhaps I should mention here, for those who do not understand the Cambridge system, that although Dr Marenbon's writings on medieval philosophy are held in good regard, he is not a member of the English Faculty. Before the public outcry of 1993 brought him media coverage many lecturers in English at Cambridge did not know his name. This presumably explains why he seemed to know so little about current debates.

Harding says that the SEAC obsession with secrecy verged on the paranoid. The famous (or infamous) Key Stage 3 anthology, which I examine later in this chapter, landed on his desk at the end of 1992 without its ever having been seen by the English committee. The English committee as a whole had nothing to do with this anthology, and Harding did not know who chose the contents. He tells how this obsession with secrecy prevented him from visiting two local schools which in November 1992 were trialling the pilot SATs for Key Stage 3. When SEAC discovered he had arranged to visit the schools, they instructed the schools not to go ahead. This meant, he says, either that SEAC had something to hide, even from the English committee, or that they had no confidence in his integrity, even though he had been invited to serve on one of SEAC's committees. Obviously Harding would have respected the confidentiality of the pilot tests. As he says, SEAC's pretence of consultation by involving teachers on an English committee was a farce. In common with many teachers who opposed the Government's education policies in 1993, Harding insisted that he was not a 'trendy lefty', but in many respects held traditional views on English studies.

Confidentiality prevents advisers and examiners from giving full information about the pilot tests for Key Stage 3 English, but enough information has emerged to show that SEAC was determined to force on teachers the tests it wanted against strong professional advice. The whole process was very expensive, and moved from disaster to disaster. Prior to the academic year 1992-3, SEAC employed three agencies (CATS, ELMAG and NEAB) to prepare pilot assessments. In the summer of 1992 SEAC and the Government rejected most of the findings of these pilots. SEAC prepared new and ill-conceived specifications for the first statutory assessments, which were put out to tender. These new specifications were the culmination of a number of abruptly introduced changes to the test specifications, presumably under the influence of Lord Griffiths. SEAC appointed as development agency a unit in the University of Cambridge Local Examinations Syndicate (UCLES) specialising in English as a Second Language. Many teachers were not surprised that SEAC should be sympathetic to an organisation which taught English as a foreign language, for the new English curriculum reflected a similarly bizarre concept of how to teach English to native speakers.

On 17 December 1992 Lord Griffiths had sent head teachers a letter about Key Stage 3 English assessment. This letter claimed that the 1993 tests (to take place on 9 June) were built on two years of trialling culminating in a pilot of 2 per cent of schools in 1992. This suggested that the development had been a continuous and cumulative process, which was not true. The 1992 specification for UCLES was quite different in form and content. The tests had been trialled in only 32 schools, amounting to approximately 0.8 per cent of all schools. Lord Griffiths's letter refers to the involvement of practising teachers in the setting, vetting and trialling of the tests. This claim was also repeatedly asserted by Baroness Blatch, the Minister of State. In fact the majority of teachers were vigorously opposed to this kind of testing, and Griffiths and Blatch were trying to suppress this truth. The statutory duties of SEAC did not include consultation with teachers, unlike those of NCC. Consequently, there was no consultation with the unions and professional associations on the development of the tests.

How not to test

Behind the scenes the early drafts prepared by UCLES caused dismay among their advisers. At a series of conferences around the country in late January 1993 SEAC introduced to a range of school teachers, LEA officers and advisers sample questions which were to be circulated to schools in February. These questions, along with the pre-tests of the actual papers to be taken in June, had been prepared by UCLES to match the specification.

The conferences expressed concern and alarm at the nature of the sample questions. Two of the conferences passed motions expressing no confidence in the tests, in particular calling in question the actual coverage of the Statutory Order for English by the test, and the general test methodology implicit in the questions.

Both NATE and NAAE published extensive papers for teachers explaining what had gone wrong. Year 9 pupils were being used as guinea pigs to try out a system of assessment which had not been properly piloted, and which did not command the respect of teachers and professionals in the field of education. The results of these tests would be used for publicly reported league tables. This proposal for 1993 league tables for Key Stages 1 and 3 was withdrawn by John Patten as a sop to English teachers when in the early months of this year the opposition to the tests was gathering strength. The tests were narrow and simplistic, and had been introduced to teachers in a confused manner. No information about the content of the papers was sent to schools until December. By this time, the year's work had been planned, according to the variety required by the 1989 English curriculum. Money available to English departments had been spent to resource the year's work, and now suddenly new Shakespeare set texts meant more money was needed. These are the simple administrative problems which further damaged teacher morale and which derived from Lord Griffiths's ignorance of what goes on in schools.

Teachers particularly objected to the imposition of 'tiers' of tests, introduced for the second specification in 1991. Teachers were forced to grade their pupils into four tiers of attainment in advance of the tests. This meant that the test papers were focussed on levels 3, 4 or 5-7 or 7-10 of the Statutory Order for English. No other set of tests yet devised by SEAC had this structure of non-overlapping papers. Weaker pupils, for example, would not be asked to study a complete Shakespeare play, but merely one passage from the Marenbon anthology which only became available early in 1993. This included Jacques's speech 'All the World's a Stage' from *As You Like It,* and a Shakespeare sonnet, number 73: 'That time of year thou mayst in me behold'. Teachers who were introducing mixed ability classes to Shakespeare were particularly incensed, for they were forced to divide sheep from goats.

Later in this chapter I quote a letter from a school to Mr Patten specifically objecting to this treatment of pupils of low ability. They would be debarred from studying a whole play, and asked to read only the Jacques speech chosen because it fitted the anthology theme of 'the journey through life'. Teachers complained that although this extract appears to give an unproblematic account of what life is like and how people behave (lovers sigh and write poetry; soldiers swear and are quarrelsome; justices are full of wise saws; old people are decrepit) in the play these trite observations are undercut by other parts of the play.

Children might think these were Shakespeare's opinions, somewhat superficial, and so he might be devalued. The strength of the passage depends to a large extent on knowing something about the apparently world-weary character who speaks the words. All Shakespeare speeches should be considered in their dramatic context, and this exercise prevented this. There were also stupid errors in the sample questions. Pupils were asked to match a quotation to a production photograph. The 'correct' answer showed Friar Lawrence looking on while Juliet poisons herself, but, of course, Friar Lawrence has departed by this point.

Such stupidities were a sign of the lack of care and the rush with which this material had been prepared. Most important, the system of 'tiers' meant that some children would be entered for the wrong tier, for SEAC had not made the criteria sufficiently clear to teachers. Teachers were not confident about carrying out this grading, and the possibility that pupils would be entered for the wrong tier invalidated the test scores. Pupils would know the tier for which they had been selected many months in advance of the test, and so there was a considerable likelihood that pupils in lower tiers would be demoralised and demotivated.

The decision to enforce this task on teachers was typical of the confusion created by people who ignore professional advice. Teachers were supposed not to be competent to assess Key Stage 3 by coursework, but they were given the great responsibility of deciding which pupils would only have the chance of a low grade.

The Key Stage 3 test in English was divided into three sections:

Paper 1: a test of reading and writing (one and a half hours)
Paper 2: a test of prior reading (one and a half hours)
Paper 3: a test of extended writing (one and a half hours)

In an article on 5 March 1993 in the *TES* Bob Bibby, previously English inspector for Dudley, argued that the Key Stage 3 tests failed to assess the current Statutory Orders, and could be legally challenged by parents. He explored the weaknesses of the sample questions by asking three questions:

- Do the questions measure what it is claimed they measure?
- Do the questions provide adequate measures of assessment of achievement in the National Curriculum statements of attainment for English?
- Do the questions validly and reliably assess achievement in English?

His answer to each question was a resounding 'No!'.

Paper 1

Paper 1, Part 1: 'Reading Comprehension' bore little relation to the statements of attainment for levels 5 - 7. The paper was designed to 'test pupils' understanding of the ideas and language contained in one or more passages.' What it actually tests, Bibby says, is '*the ability to interpret the meaning of the questions, the ability to copy chunks of text appropriately, the ability to produce synonyms, the ability to spot a metaphor but not to comment on its force, and the ability to guess what is in the examiner's mind.*' This form of assessing understanding of written texts had been widely discredited by the bulk of research into reading, which stresses the part played by the individual reader in lifting meaning from texts. This fault in the tests is of great importance, because it brings out once more how the rejection of professional advice by government ministers was damaging the heart of English as a subject. For many years exciting developments in literary theory (in the writings of Stanley Fish or Wolfgang Iser, for example) have involved an examination of reader response, and good teachers have encouraged their pupils to develop their own readings. If pupils and students are made to repeat the response of the teacher, or to try to answer questions according to what they think the teacher wants, then the result may well be a form of hypocrisy. This applies both to the reading tests in Paper 1 and to Paper 2, the Literature paper. As a senior citizen my views of *Romeo and Juliet*, for example, are not likely to resemble those of a fourteen-year-old. These questions of what is a 'correct' response lead into controversial areas, because pupils must not be allowed to get away with readings which are palpably wrong. But in the teaching and assessment of reading only professionals can gauge what is appropriate. What dismayed the teaching profession in 1993 was that assessment was in the control of people who were not even aware of the arguments.

Paper 1, Part 2: 'Use of Language' was similarly inappropriate. This paper was designed to 'test pupils' knowledge of the correct use of language' by assessing their 'ability to make appropriate lexical choices' and their 'use of grammar'. What it actually tests, Bibby says, is '*the ability to produce synonyms (again), the ability to guess the words chosen by the author, or those identified by the examiner as acceptable, and the ability to play language games.*'

Exercises where a pupil is asked to find lexical alternatives or to play language games are not likely to produce accurate assessments. When I joined the army in 1947 I took a test which provided us with a number of definitions and then asked us to complete for each definition a word beginning with PAR. One definition was 'a heavenly place'. I wrote

'Parnassus', and was cross when I was told the correct answer was 'Paradise'. I was being too clever, and should have considered more carefully what the examiner was likely to require, a common problem for able students when faced with multiple-choice or language game tests under examination conditions.

In examining use of language, coursework *must* be included in the process of assessment. Through coursework pupils can develop their own meanings, and proceed through drafts, the normal process for a professional writer. This is particularly relevant to Paper 1, Part 3: 'Directed Writing'. This paper was designed so that pupils can 'show their ability to write correctly and to organise their writing'. Bibby comments:

> What it actually tests is the ability to write for a 'pretend' audience, with no details of its origination or address, and the ability to engage with a writing task unrelated to previous classroom work, to the pupils' own interests, or to the real needs of their own school. Consequently the task lacks real or meaningful audience, purpose or context.

Paper 2

Paper 2: 'Test of Prior Reading' was designed to assess 'understanding of plot, character and setting, appreciation of prose and poetry, and a personal response to the texts read'. What it actually tests, Bibby says, '*is the ability to recall facts, the ability to answer comprehension questions, the ability to demonstrate appreciation by making preferences, the ability to reproduce conventional readings of texts, the ability to produce synonyms (again), the opportunity to achieve success in reading without reading a whole book, and the opportunity to treat reading as a game.*' In all these papers the right-wing wanted to examine complete, fixed responses determined by the authority of the teacher or examiner. There is a fear of variety, individuality and imagination. The questions, Bibby says, had been '*set on the premise that there are fixed responses, which are either right or wrong, that these responses can be numerically indicated ("Give three reasons", etc) and that the reading and understanding of literary texts is unproblematic and straightforward.*' The treatment of Shakespeare particularly enraged good teachers. The written tests would demand detailed knowledge of the plots, characters and vocabulary. Such tests encourage boring context and comprehension exercises, the learning by rote of the happenings in acts and scenes, and the dishonesties of prepared answers as students parrot what they have been told will get them good marks.

Paper 3

Paper 3: 'Test of Extended Writing' was also old-fashioned and dull. The test was designed to 'cover aspects of writing skills such as range of expression, clarity of communication, coverage of content and correct use of language'. Bibby comments: '*What it actually tests is the ability to write interestingly about one of a set of drab and uninspiring titles, the ability to write without any clear notion of the audience being written for, the ability to write on complex issues without any access to research materials or other resources, and the ability to compose a piece of writing without going through a drafting process.*'

The *TES* of 5 March 1993 included twelve pages of attacks on the tests. A cartoon summed up their mechanical nature; a bemused student was being asked: '*Why did Romeo fall in love with Juliet? Give three reasons.*' When I worked as an examiner for the old 'O' level examination, we were confronted with the problem of how many marks to award to an easy context question on some well-known words spoken by Lady Macbeth. Two marks were allocated for 'Lady Macbeth', but we were then asked whether a pupil who missed out 'Lady' should receive any reward. To my amazement, it was decided to allocate one mark. Such absurdities were rife forty years ago when examinations in literature for sixteen-year-olds usually included large numbers of context questions. When I took the old school certificate in 1944, I was able to complete the whole literature paper by answering context questions, and so earn a distinction. Whether I enjoyed or understood or had any original ideas about the texts were irrelevant considerations. These were the golden days to which Lord Griffiths harked back nostalgically in his plans for assessment. By the time 'O' level was dropped it was a discredited examination. Many schools would not allow pupils to enter for it, as its approach to literature was too narrow, asking little but basic comprehension and a knowledge of the story line of a very few books. In 1972 the number of school leavers with 'O' level English Literature was a small fraction of the number of those with Chemistry.

In 1993 the indignation and dismay of teachers brought them out in droves to attend meeings and to campaign for a boycott of the tests. In the *TES* of 5 March Sue Hackman contributed an excellent essay on the underlying assumptions of the new assessment system and why English teachers were so angry. In recent decades British education has moved from a knowledge-based to a skills-based model. The common core in the Cox curriculum is defined as much in terms of shared competencies as shared facts. The factual content remains important, of course, but this is seen as justified largely in helping students to solve problems. Sue

Hackman was an advisory teacher in Surrey, and had recently resigned her post as a chief assessor for Key Stage 3. She wrote:

> The tests challenge the prevailing ethos of teachers by assuming a model of education in which learning is passive, absolute and knowledge-based. In this model, snapshot tests are intended to reveal the amount of learning which has been achieved.
>
> English teachers are more inclined to see learning as personal and provisional, gradually consolidated on to previous understandings. In other words, learning is recursive. In this model, each learner will take a different route to understanding, appropriate to his or her experience and aptitude, and the prime purpose of assessment is to identify the optimum conditions of progress.

In the SEAC assessments the pupils were confined to the kind of tests where they fill in the gaps. This kind of reading sees textual meanings as fixed, and demands conformity of interpretation. For English teachers each reading is formed of an interaction of reader, text and cultural context, and modified when it is shared and challenged among the wider reading community. Sue Hackman explained that teachers *'who now see themselves as guiding and intervening in individual development are being required to convert to a transmission style of teaching, seeing themselves much more as custodians of, and inductors into, established knowledge.'* These words bring out once more why this dispute was much more than a disagreement about methods of assessment. Two concepts of the pupil and society were at war. The right-wingers wanted to impose their own concept of an English identity and culture on all the nation's children. The English teachers wanted to encourage independence and honesty of response.

The Key Stage 3 English Anthology

These deep-seated attitudes were reflected in the choice of excerpts for the extraordinary anthology published by SEAC in the first week of January 1993 on which fourteen-year-olds were to be tested in the summer. To the lay person at first glance the choice of texts might seem unexceptional if somewhat predictable, but in fact the selection brought out why the interference of right-wingers was likely to be so damaging to educational standards. The main influence was Dr Marenbon, who acknowledged that he had been involved in oversight of the preparation of the anthology, but claimed that the contractors - UCLES - and SEAC officials had drafted the list after consultations. The anthology included the Shakespeare passages I have already mentioned, an extract from Chaucer ('The Knight and the Squire', both in the original and a modern translation), excerpts from Dickens's *David Copperfield*, Johnson's *Rasselas*, Wilde's *The Importance of Being Earnest*, Laurie Lee's *Cider with Rosie* and Dylan Thomas's *A Child's Christmas in Wales*. Famous poems were included such as Blake's *Infant Sorrow*, Wordsworth's *Daffodils*, Keats's *To Autumn*, Browning's *Home Thoughts from Abroad* and Edward Thomas's *Adlestrop*, plus a sprinkling of more recent poets such as Philip Larkin (*At Grass*), Anthony Thwaite (*A Haiku Yearbook*), Elizabeth Jennings (*My Grandmother*), Patricia Pogson (*Yesterday*) and R. S. Thomas (*Cynddylan on a Tractor*). Obeisance to writers in English from outside Britain was confined to a short story by Doris Lessing and a poem by Derek Walcott. Derek Walcott's poem is *The Young Wife*, about cancer, not exactly an obvious choice for a teacher trying to arouse enthusiasm in a recalcitrant thirteen-year-old.

Teachers immediately pointed out that there was a major misprint in the Dickens excerpt, for the word 'Ham' in the last paragraph should have been 'Him' to refer to the villainous Mr Murdstone. It also turned out that the passage had been abridged, with thirty paragraphs cut after the opening paragraph in which David tells Emily he loves her, thus making the second paragraph absurdly distorted. Why should pupils be forced to read Dickens in this corrupt version? This cock-up was typical of events in 1993.

Teachers objected that it was not clear what kinds of questions the extracts would generate. The 'Guide for Teachers' allocated the passages to tiered clusters of national curriculum levels in a complex way which could never lead to accurate assessment. Lord Griffiths said that the anthology had been released early to help teachers plan, but '*there is absolutely no need for teachers to use it with their pupils until the last few weeks before the tests. The last thing we want to do is encourage schools simply to teach to the test.*' (*TES*, 8 January 1993). For anyone with even the minimum understanding of schools these remarks are unbelievably naive. Teachers are judged by the performance of their pupils in tests, and however noble their intentions and ideals this pressure is difficult to resist. Any teachers worried about their standing in a school would obviously want to impart a thorough knowledge of the passages as soon as possible.

Perhaps most absurd was the decision that pupils expected to reach only levels 3 or 4 should be faced by Jacques's 'All the World's a Stage' speech. I have already discussed how the speech should not be taken at face value, but is an expression of an Elizabethan malcontent, in contrast to the comic exuberance of much of the rest of the play. Obviously these pupils were to be denied any joy in Shakespearian drama, and made to learn the meaning of words in the speech off by heart.

But the major objection to the anthology was that it reflected nostalgia for a lost golden age of pastoral bliss. In a typically witty review 'Back to the future', in *Education* (22 January 1993), Graham Frater wrote:

> Where it is not gloomy, the collection is bland. Some adults will find this refreshing. Nostalgia runs as a rich vein through the rest of the assortment: *A Child's Christmas in Wales, Home Thoughts from Abroad, Adlestrop, Daffodils.* The mood is so relentlessly retrospective that even the youngest living writer (date of birth 1944) is represented by a poem entitled *Yesterday.* And whatever their individual virtues, the landscape pieces - surely there are too many - depict idealised scenes in a Georgian mode. Their vistas are hardly peopled at all, but there is much play with those sensations which may safely be prompted in solitary poets by scenery and weather. So little does the present century obtrude on the rural idyll that when a modern machine is featured (Cynddylan's tractor), it is in a poem which views it rather loftily as corrupting the character of the peasantry.

Frater points out how the poems in the anthology include none of those areas of life most likely to resonate with the adolescent reader, such as young love, generational conflict or the tensions between self and society.

Much has been written about nostalgia as a dominating trait in both English literature and literary criticism in the twentieth century. I presume Dr Marenbon was unaware of these debates. Particularly well-known is Paul Fussell's *The Great War and Modern Memory* (1975). Fussell shows how in many writings about the 1914-18 war, such as the prose works of Siegfried Sassoon or David Jones's *In Parenthesis* (1937), the artist reaches out for traditional significance, attempts to re-attach traditional meanings to the unprecedented actualities of war. Trench warfare is meaningless and nauseating; language is used by many English writers to re-assert English cultural identity by using images of pastoral continuity or by employing the connectives of grammar, rhyme and rhythm as a form of resistance to disorder. I wrote about this at length in

1991 in 'English Studies and National Identity' (published in Mike Hayhoe and Stephen Parker (eds), *Reassessing Language and Literacy*, 1992). Fussell shows how the nostalgic impulse works as an important agency in adjustment to crisis, a social emollient that reinforces national identity when confidence is weakened or threatened. In the 1950s the reaction against modernism in 'Movement' poets such as Philip Larkin often resorted to this kind of nostalgia (as in his poem *MCMXIV*). F. R. Leavis's nostalgia for the so-called organic community of the English village in pre-industrial England is a comparable phenomenon, a distaste for modern society. The nostalgia among many English readers for comic characters in fiction, from the Wife of Bath to Falstaff to Pickwick to Jeeves, reflects a desire for a world under control, for the reduction of personal and social conflict to humorous entertainment. This is a feature of many audiences at amateur theatre productions who do not wish to be disturbed by Beckett or Pinter or Joe Orton or David Hare.

Many university teachers expressed their disgust for the anthology. In 'Insults to the Intelligence' (Letters, *The Journal of the Royal Society of Literature*, Spring 1993), John Carey, Merton Professor of English Literature at Oxford, complained about the 'alarming meagreness of this selection'. He was shocked to discover that pupils were not expected to have the stamina to read even this pathetic pamphlet from cover to cover. They were only asked to 'become familiar with' just seven of the texts, and teachers must ensure that of these seven they have 'studied' four 'core texts' for the test. Carey repeated the point I have already made that the devisers of this scheme fell into the well-known trap of forgetting that teachers would be forced to concentrate only on the requirements of the test, and wider reading would be neglected. Setting this booklet for study would diminish the chance of other books being read, or even looked at. Children must be free to read widely and indiscriminately, devouring reams of what their parents and mentors may well consider trash. This prescribed anthology would destroy any sense of exploration by the inquisitive pupil. Professor Carey commented:

> Teachers have also complained that the choice of texts in the anthology is likely to bore or antagonise the children for whom it is designed. Here, too, they seem to be right. You could scarcely hit on a poem more likely to strike most thirteen-year-olds as soppy than Wordsworth's *Daffodils*, and to children at that stage of development the extremely adult wit of Wilde's *The Importance of Being Earnest* will mean absolutely nothing. The 'Guide for Teachers' tells us that the pieces in the anthology were meant to

illustrate two 'linked themes', the seasons (*Daffodils, To Autumn,* etc) and the journey through life (Chaucer's Knight and Squire, 'All the World's a Stage').

The trouble is that it would take quite a lot of ingenuity to select two themes more calculated to fill thirteen-year-olds with total indifference. At that age children are notoriously blind to what adults think of as 'natural beauty' and they have no interest whatever in getting old. You might-as well try to sell them life insurance policies. (p.23)

After the success of the Key Stage 3 boycott in 1993 this anthology was quietly forgotten. Once again a large amount of money had been wasted which could have been spent on school libraries.

Parents and teachers

In the early weeks of 1993 the campaign to boycott the tests grew apace. By 3 February the London Association for the Teaching of English (LATE) could announce that over 700 schools had declared their intention to join the boycott. Although the reasons for the boycott were mainly professional disgust at the shoddy, crude nature of the tests, and anger at the administrative chaos with which they had been introduced, John Patten fuelled the flames by his extraordinary public pronouncements. At the end of January he called the parents who opposed the tests 'neanderthal', and he described the opposition as well-orchestrated by union militants and the Marxist establishment. In April he told school governors they had a legal duty to ensure the tests took place. Governors' leaders replied that they would not be intimidated by threats to coerce them to discipline teachers, and that such action would bring disillusionment and deter people from serving as governors. The National Association of Governors and Managers advised its members not to discipline teachers who took part in boycotts, unless they acted illegally.

In an article on 16 February in the *Guardian* Peter Thomas, head of English at Wheatley Park School, Oxfordshire, spoke for almost all teachers of English when he accused John Patten of 'denying my vocation'. He wrote:

❛ I chose to be a teacher because I love books and I enjoy working with young people. I enjoy seeing youngsters involved in performing Shakespeare. I enjoy their pride in their writing. I'm pleased when we push up our exam successes in competition with neighbour schools. I like to see pupils' success in public exams take them on to further study. Make no mistake about it, they worked harder under 100 per cent coursework than youngsters have ever worked.

The words of this typical enthusiastic teacher once again illustrate the great divide between the reality of schools and the fantasies about Marxism and hatred for exams which filled the mind of John Patten and followers such as Dr John Marks. It soon became apparent that large numbers of parents supported the teachers and knew they were not left-wing loonies. Meetings of parents and teachers were held all over the country to discuss the tests and the boycott. The political importance of this sympathy for teachers became apparent when in the spring the Conservatives lost the Newbury bye-election; Conservative canvassers discovered on the doorstep that large numbers of voters were seriously worried about Mr Patten's confrontation with the teachers and feared he was doing harm to the education of their children.

From April onwards the opposition grew apace. On 2 April the *TES* reported that meetings to support the boycott were taking place even in schools in the Conservative heartlands. Margaret Morrissey, spokeswoman for the National Confederation of Parent-Teacher Associations, confirmed that there was a groundswell of parents pulling their children out of tests: '*Parents are saying our children are being used as guinea-pigs. We have had change after change in our schools and quite frankly we have had enough.*'

In the last week of April, John Patten launched a £700,000 campaign to convince parents of the virtues of the tests. A leaflet for parents was sent to every school in England, and a series of advertisements were placed in national newspapers and magazines. Ann Taylor, Labour's education spokeswoman, called this publicity campaign 'an offensive abuse of taxpayers' money'. The campaign had a reverse effect, for many parents were antagonised to see so much money spent to defend tests they knew were unsuited to their children's needs.

In the first week of May a poll of parental opinion, carried out by NOP for the *Independent* (10 May), confirmed that most parents with children of school age believed the Government should abandon the 1993 National Curriculum tests, and, to the surprise of Ministers, that two-thirds thought that tests for seven-year-olds should be scrapped altogether. All the parents interviewed had children aged between 5 and 16. Just over half said they supported the teachers' boycott of the tests scheduled for the summer term, while only 27 per cent actively opposed the boycott: the remainder were undecided and uncommitted. Only 31 per cent thought that Ministers should press ahead with this year's tests, against 62 per cent who thought they should be dropped. A poll conducted by Gallup for the *Daily Telegraph* (10 May) found that 62 per cent of voters thought the tests were too time-consuming and complicated, and 77 per cent thought the Government's education reforms had been introduced too quickly. Only 19 per cent thought Mr Patten was doing a good job.

A parents' campaign against tests had already achieved considerable success in Scotland. A compromise had been agreed in the New Year in 1993 after two years of boycotts by parents and teachers. The Scottish system was a voluntary agreement between the Scottish Office and the country's twelve education authorities. There were five stages of attainment covering the 5 - 14 curriculum, and pupils were tested only when their teacher judged them ready to move on to the next stage. This means that testing is generally done only in small groups and at any time of the year. Children are not tested every year, and results only go to parents and school boards. There are no league tables. In May, Raymond Boyle, a founder member of the Scottish Parents' Coalition, which discovered that up to 80 per cent of parents were opposed to national tests and engineered a massive boycott, reported that he was receiving calls from parents throughout England and Wales who opposed the tests. Ann Taylor of the Labour Party expressed sympathy with the Scottish approach.

New organisations and alignments emerged, as teachers and parents of conflicting political beliefs found they were at one in their opposition to Mr Patten. An interesting feature of political life at this time was that opposition to Conservative policies was often organised by professional groups rather than by the Labour Party. The Labour Party feared to be labelled as progressives who opposed all testing and did not care about basics, and so throughout these campaigns the behaviour of most left-wing politicians was pusillanimous.

A National Campaign against SATs had been started two years previously, and in the stirring times of 1993 it pushed itself to the fore with numerous press statements. Circulars were sent out from its office in South East London to all chairs of school governors. This organisation claimed to be a national 'parent-led' network actively supporting parents in several parts of England who wished to withdraw their children from testing. A powerful organisation of head teachers and deputies was set up specifically in response to the management and assessment problems created by Key Stage 3. This was called the National Co-ordinating Committee on Learning and Assessment (NCCLA), and soon it began to organise conferences and publish pamphlets. Its secretary, Hugh Benjamin, deputy head at Stantonbury Campus grant-maintained school in Milton Keynes, supported parents who withdrew their children from the tests (interview in the *TES* on 9 April).

Mike Lloyd, head of English at Bourneville School in Birmingham, organised a spectacular campaign to save English coursework at GCSE after the Prime Minister announced in July 1991 the curtailment of coursework assessment to a maximum of 40 per cent. Every head of English in more than 4,000 state secondaries and larger independent schools was asked if they supported the campaign to call for grades to be calculated on the basis of 80 per cent coursework and 20 per cent on a final exam. Almost three-quarters replied, with an overwhelming majority - 96 per cent - in favour of the proposal. Just 24 of the 2,902 responses were in favour of the Government's changes, while 84 would settle for marking based on half coursework, half external examination. As with the Key Stage 3 assessments, the Government had reduced coursework in GCSE without consultation with schools, governors, teachers or parents. The extraordinary support for the Birmingham initiative proves that almost the entire profession of English teachers was opposed to Mr Patten.

All this activity was accompanied by numerous letters and petitions sent to Mr Patten and other MPs. Some sent copies to me. A letter from Driffield School, North Humberside, was sent on 23 November 1992 signed by eleven English teachers. They specifically attacked the decision to confine testing of a Shakespeare play to the more able students at Key Stage 3:

❝ ... we teach Shakespeare to all children beginning in Year 8, and have done so successfully for many years. We were delighted when such teaching became compulsory under the National Curriculum. Consequently our shock was the greater when information about the SATs for KS3 revealed that Shakespeare was not after all to be shared with all, but only with those thought capable of entry for the two top 'tiers'. The effect in the classroom can be of only two kinds: that we 'stream'; or that we teach to all and then demonstrate to some that their experience is not worthy of assessment (advice offered by SEAC when approached with our dilemma).

This letter represents views expressed to me by many teachers of English. In contrast to Dr Marks's fantasy about English teachers not wanting to teach Shakespeare, a major objection to the Key Stage 3 tests was that they would reduce the number of pupils studying Shakespeare (as well as making the teaching less successful).

A letter to Mr Patten from Newland School for Girls, Kingston-upon-Hull, of 24 March 1993, called the English tests 'unsound, expensive and irrelevant'. The letter, signed by seven teachers from the Faculty of Recreative and Creative Arts, drew attention to the effect of the Key Stage 3 tests on the timetable:

❢ In addition to the well-documented fact that the tests serve no real educational purpose for those pupils taking them (except to disrupt their timetable for two weeks) they will, in fact, seriously interrupt the education of the rest of the school population. In our school this means that the Performing Arts programme and sports programme will be totally disrupted. There will be no school assemblies, no visits from theatre groups or guest speakers. Our rehearsals for our traditional whole school end of year performance will be decimated. Both staff and pupils will suffer. Why is this the case? Because, in order to accommodate these tests, all the large spaces in school, namely the Gym, the Main Hall, and an annex (some distance from the main building) will have to be used and all the lessons and the hundreds of pupils which normally occupy those spaces will be ousted. Incidentally, the annex will have to be policed by staff (another extra duty) because it is subject to intrusion by youths.

Add to this the cost in human time and effort of invigilation, organisation and extra marking of hundreds of scripts. To say nothing of the time and effort to re-timetable the rest of the school and move hundreds of heavy desks and chairs by hand.

This is an important letter because it describes the nitty-gritty problems of administering exams. All schools could provide similar illustrations of what happens when exams of national importance are imposed on schools. As we move forward to the SATs of the later 1990s, such problems remain. This letter illustrates why the National Curriculum should be in the charge of people with either teaching experience in schools or knowledge of education administration. It illustrates why for Key Stages 1 to 3 the Scottish system is so superior.

The boycott was supported by the independent schools. Already in January 1993 Robin Wilson, chairman of the Headmasters' Conference, which represents the leading boys' public schools, had insisted that opposition to the tests was on educational not political grounds. Robin Wilson, head of Trinity School, Croydon, and Joan Jefferson, President of the Girls' School Association and head of St Swithun's School, Winchester, jointly published an important letter on 22 April 1993 in *The Times*. They accepted the concept of a national curriculum, but shared the deep concerns of their colleagues in state education about the testing regime being imposed. They represented schools for whom regular testing and reporting to parents are normal procedures, and they took for granted all schools should do the same. They continued:

❝ We cannot, however, accept that a national system of unified testing is anything but a cumbersome weapon, and one which inhibits good teaching both by the nature of the tests imposed, and by the excessive time taken by the whole process of testing and recording. Good schools do it much more effectively with much less interruption of the teaching programme, and much more appropriately for their particular pupils.

It is implausible to believe that one examination can fulfil three distinct functions: to act as a diagnostic tool for each pupil, to give a true picture of the school's effectiveness, and to give a national snapshot of standards. All these aims are achievable, but by different methods. We believe that this confusion of purpose is at the heart of the problem, and is also central to the objections to the crudity of the so-called league tables as a measure of the academic effectiveness of a school in bringing the best out of its pupils.

We believe that a more productive route would be to insist that all schools should adopt agreed good practice and that their testing arrangements should be carefully scrutinised. The machinery to achieve this has been put into place by the government by the institution of a regular and rigorous inspection programme.

I agree entirely with this, and I believe that the cost and muddle involved in national exams at 7, 11 and 14 will make a solution of this kind inevitable. I strongly support regular testing for diagnostic purposes and to give information to parents, but league tables at 7, 11 and 14 create too many administrative problems.

Unions and the law

Most public attention in 1993 was focussed not on the revisions of the English curriculum but on the teachers' threatened boycott of the summer tests, particularly when the NASUWT won its case in the High Court against the London Borough of Wandsworth. The Union had balloted its members with a carefully worded question which concentrated entirely on the workload aspect, and a few weeks later

Wandsworth applied to the High Court for an injunction to stop the NASUWT boycott. It was decided that the case should have a full hearing in the High Court, and this began on 31 March. The Judge, Mr Justice Mantell, insisted that if teachers were to have a statutory duty to administer the assessments and testing for the National Curriculum this should be stated in the 1988 Education Act, not in the various Orders which flowed from it. If Parliament had intended to impose a statutory duty on teachers it would have put it in the primary legislation, and, to quote the Judge, 'not have slipped a knife between the ribs of teachers' by placing such an important duty in minor statutory orders (see Eamonn O'Kane's 'Judgement Day' in *Teaching Today*, the NASUWT journal, no. 5, Summer 1993, for the full story). The case went to the Appeal Court on 20 April 1993, when the Wandsworth counsel concentrated his argument solely on the contention that this was not a dispute wholly or mainly about workload, but that the real issue at the heart of the dispute was the teachers' professional objections to the nature of the assessment and testing arrangements. The NASUWT's ballot which had carefully stressed workload won them the case. On 23 April the Appeal Court declared the dispute was a trades dispute within the meaning of the legislation, and that the NASUWT was, therefore, entitled to the immunities granted to unions under the legislation. The other unions followed suit, and the summer boycott affected almost every state school in the country.

Nigel de Gruchy, General Secretary of the NASUWT, claimed that this success restored teachers' sense of professional pride, and provided a tremendous boost to morale. It was certainly a great triumph, and I describe the consequences later as members of SEAC and NCC were replaced or resigned. But when Sir Ron Dearing took over a combined NCC and SEAC, his main remit was to deal with the workload problem and to slim down the curriculum. Attention was directed away from the faults of the English curriculum. When in September 1993 the revised English curriculum was published it attracted little attention, even when it was made the basis for the slimmed-down curriculum of 1994.

A model for Key Stage 3 English

My own ideas for English Key Stage 3 testing were put under public scrutiny when on 4 May 1993 the NUT asked me to prepare alternatives to the tests proposed by the Government. In his letter sending me this invitation, Michael Barber, Assistant Secretary, Education, of NUT, insisted that the Union's 1993 assessment campaign was underpinned by its longer term support for the Scottish assessment model: a diagnostic model based on the professional judgment of the teacher to test pupils at an appropriate point, using a bank of assessment materials for moderating requirements. The NUT, of course, was anxious to convey to the public that the Union was not opposed to testing in principle, but was sure the Government's tests were educationally damaging. I consulted widely among professional examiners who had been involved in the trials for Key Stage 3, and my proposals were published on 4 June, just before the boycott of the tests was due to take place. I print the document below, which begins with my elaboration of the points made by Robin Wilson and Joan Jefferson in their letter to *The Times*. I have cut out only the sections which repeat material included elsewhere in this book.

Introduction

1 Good teachers are strongly in favour of assessment and testing. The problem is to ensure that the process does not interfere with the real educational needs of children. The present arrangements for Key Stage 3 English are damaging real education, and that is why we are hearing such fierce protests from pupils, parents, teachers and governors.

Purposes of Assessment

2 Current assessment is supposed to fulfil three main purposes. In public debate during the last year these three aims have continually been muddled. They are:

(a) *Diagnostic.* This helps teachers to evaluate the strengths and weaknesses of pupils, and to plan strategies to benefit individual and class learning. Diagnostic tests give pupils and parents information about achievements, and help them to assess progress.

(b) *League Tables.* These are intended to help parents judge their school's performance against local and national standards.

(c) *Assessment of National Standards.* This can produce data on whether standards of spelling or reading, for example, are rising or falling.

3 Assessment of national standards can be done by well-planned sampling, and this has been carried out in the past by the now defunct Assessment of Performance Unit. There is no need for every child to be assessed, and so this aim is irrelevant for Key Stage 3 testing.

4 Diagnostic assessment is essential to monitor the individual pupil's progress, and to provide guidance for the future. The demands of this kind of testing are often in conflict with the demands imposed by league tables. There are three main reasons why there should be no league tables for Key Stage 3:

(a) *Expense.* A national system of monitoring will cost millions of pounds per year. The money would be better spent on books for children or other educational needs.

(b) *Inaccuracy.* The recently devised system in which fourteen-year-olds are tested in order to produce league tables will have many teething problems, and will certainly be inaccurate for many years. League tables in such circumstances will be meaningless. Parents are against league tables for Key Stage 3 because they recognise they will be misleading. In the poll published in the *Independent* on 10 May parents were asked: '*In the future if all schools do take part in the tests, do you think the overall test results for each school should be published as a sort of league table of schools' achievement, or would any such tables be misleading?*' The results were:

Publish table	27 per cent
Table misleading	70 per cent
Don't know	3 per cent

(c) *Inappropriate Assessment.* The best kind of assessment of English often depends on impression marking. It is difficult to standardise, and disparities at Key Stage 3 between schools are inevitable. Advocates of KS3 league tables have therefore put pressure on SEAC for simple tests in which pupils score one point for answers that can be marked right or wrong. There is also pressure for multiple-choice tests. These simple tests can lead to bad teaching. For example, testing of a prescribed Shakespeare play which asks for explanation of words or phrases, or for the precise context of a speech, leads to boring lessons during which the class go through the play again and again *ad nauseam.* This kind of testing kills enthusiasm for Shakespeare by making pupils learn simply the superficial meanings of words and the order in which scenes take place or characters enter the action. The dramatic and poetic richness of language, action or characterisation are undervalued, as such qualities are not amenable to right/wrong questioning. If teachers are forced to teach for the test because they will be judged by league tables, they are made to abandon more enriching educational activities.

Methods of Assessment

5 Course assessment is particularly appropriate for many vital activities in the study of English language and literature:

(a) *Speaking and Listening.* Timed tests might be possible for a formal presentation, such as a lecture, but Speaking and Listening should be almost entirely assessed through less formal activities in class. Assessment must cover the range of situations and activities which should take place over a period of time within natural teaching contexts. It is vital that Speaking and Listening should be assessed, because otherwise they will be downgraded. Experiments in assessment are continuing, but valuable work has already been carried out, both since 1990 at Key Stage 3 and since 1986 in relation to GCSE.

(b) *Reading from a range of texts in a variety of genres.* Pupils need to read widely and with enthusiasm. This can be assessed by the teacher through tasks in which the pupil chooses a variety of texts for commentary and evaluation as part of a folder submitted for assessment. The anthology set for Key Stage 3 in 1993 was a disaster for classroom teaching because it limited pupils to the reading mainly of excerpts and short poems which were often inappropriate for this age group and which reflected a narrow range of sensibility.

(c) *Writing.* Good writers normally achieve their final product after revision of drafts and after advice from their peers. This activity is crucial in developing writing skills, and is not best tested in one-hour timed exams. It is also difficult to create real, or even moderately convincing, contexts for writing in a short, timed test, whereas writing in class can become an integral part of an activity with real outcomes, such as writing genuine letters which are sent to actual people in the expectation of obtaining a reply, writing stories for use in primary schools, writing a guide to the school for new pupils, etc.

(d) *Drama.* Drama is an important means of developing and broadening pupils' verbal communication. It has become a vital element in the imaginative teaching of literature. In recent years emphasis on dramatic activities in classrooms has been welcomed by the business community. Role play in which participants present cases to different audiences is a normal part of business training. Drama activities have to be teacher-assessed.

(e) Knowledge about Language. In the present English Orders KAL is an important thread running through the profile components. Teachers have welcomed its intellectual challenge; it is best taught through long-term projects in class.

(f) Media. Pupils need to be taught to evaluate the use of language and presentational devices in the media as part of their awareness of specific English skills. This is best accomplished using real examples in the classroom where discussion and debate may take place, rather than expecting simplistic right/wrong answers to previously unseen material in a timed test.

The Revised English Orders
6 Models for assessment of English depend on what happens to the revised NCC English Orders. These revisions have been almost totally rejected by the profession. (This section of my NUT document continued with reasons for the rejection which have already been discussed at length in this book.)

Proposed Model of Assessment
7 In the model for Key Stage 3 English presented in this paper 80 per cent of marks are allocated to teacher assessment and 20 per cent to externally set Standard Assessment Tasks tested under timed examination conditions. The model could easily be adapted to 60 per cent for teacher assessment and 40 per cent for timed exams, if the Government insists. Almost all teachers of English would welcome the freedom to promote high standards in speaking, listening, reading and writing offered by a system in which 80 per cent of marks are teacher-assessed. When the Save English Coursework campaign polled heads of English, a large majority were in favour of the 80:20 model.

8 The 80:20 per cent proposal is a response to the present political climate. In the long run there are strong arguments for moving towards the systems of assessment of fourteen- year-olds in place in independent schools and in Scotland. (This section of the NUT document continued with description and a quotation from the letter of Robin Wilson and Joan Jefferson in *The Times*.) In Scotland there is no intention that schools will be ranked on the basis of national tests. The national tests are selected by teachers from a catalogue of tests on a variety of topics, prepared by groups of teachers in working parties under the Scottish Examination

Board. Tests take place when the teacher's own assessment indicates that the pupil has largely achieved the statements of attainment at one level, and is ready to move from that level to the next in that aspect, irrespective of the stage or time of year. This system is working well in Scotland, and should be carefully considered for adoption in England and Wales as soon as possible.

9 The proposed model would be available for all pupils, and there would be no need to separate them into tiers.

(a) Speaking and Listening. 20 per cent of marks to be allocated to this component. Testing entirely by teacher assessment.

(b) Reading. 40 per cent of marks to be allocated to this component. 30 per cent by teacher assessment which will cover prior reading as laid down in the Programmes of Study; 10 per cent by externally set SAT under timed examination conditions, targeting by 'spot test' those statements of attainment most amenable to this kind of test.

(c) Writing. 40 per cent of marks to be allocated to this component. 30 per cent by teacher assessment involving both informative and imaginative writing; 10 per cent by externally set SAT under timed examination conditions eliciting both informative and imaginative writing.

10 This model would allow pupils:

(a) to participate in speaking and listening activities so that these retain a crucial role in the assessment process. Advice on appropriate activities could be prepared by test agencies. Integrated tasks could also assess knowledge about language.

(b) to engage with a range of texts, including Shakespeare, pre-1900 classics, writings in English from different cultures, and media texts, rather than a few prescribed texts tested in timed exams. The written test in exam conditions would assess close reading and response; it would assess every pupils' ability to transfer certain skills to the understanding of unseen texts. Range and enjoyment of reading, and a considered response, cannot be tested in timed conditions or by simple objective questions.

(c) to submit completed writing assignments which have been drafted and redrafted. Pupils would undertake a range of writing tasks with a variety of audiences in mind, with a strong emphasis on the need to convey meaning clearly, effectively and imaginatively.

11 Spelling, punctuation and grammar would be assessed through both teacher assessment and the test papers. Assessment would be based on the pupils' use of language in real tasks as opposed to spelling, vocabulary and grammar exercises.

12 Teacher assessment would be moderated and standardised by groups of teachers. This is particularly valuable for in-service training. Banks of possible assignments would be made available to teachers. Record-keeping would have to be carefully structured and clear.

13 *Test/Assignments*. There should be 2 x 1 hour papers taken under timed exam conditions.

Paper 1: 10 per cent. Short, linked literary passages for close reading and response, comparison, etc.

If a paper for pupils consisted of two poems such as Thomas Hardy's *Snow in the Suburbs* and Edward Thomas's *Snow*, pupils might be asked to:

♦ describe the feeling captured in the poems;
♦ explain the effects of the different rhyme/rhythm schemes;
♦ generally contrast and compare the poets' approaches to the subject;
♦ support a preference for one or other of the texts.

Prompts would both assist pupils and ensure that responses were directed towards statements of attainment addressed in the mark scheme. Poems would be ones pupils had not seen before, so their response would be based on long-term teaching of a wide range of poetry, rather than on 'coaching' of specific poems.

Paper 2: 10 per cent. Non-literary stimulus material for directed writing task involving re-presentation.

Pupils might be presented with a leaflet or 'flyer' describing an event: They are then asked to write an account of that event for a school newspaper, using:

♦ appropriate content;
♦ appropriate vocabulary and grammar;
♦ suitable presentational devices, etc.

Again, prompts concerning those aspects would ensure some relationship between the outcome and the statements of attainment and the mark scheme.

14 Course Assessment. Four assigments.
(a) An assignment on Shakespeare - *20 per cent.*
(b) An assignment on poetry - *20 per cent.*
(c) An assignment on fiction - *20 per cent.*
(d) An assignment on non-literary and media texts - *20 per cent.*

15 Examples of assignments on Shakespeare. Teachers would be free to choose their own Shakespearian texts. Test agencies would provide clear advice on tasks. The following notes indicate the kind of work which would be part of the assignment for pupils who studied *Julius Caesar* or *Romeo and Juliet.*

Julius Caesar
(a) An Activity. Pupils in groups would prepare and take part in a dramatic presentation of the assassination scene or the murder of Cinna the poet. Children of all levels of ability would contribute.
(b) Discussion. Pupils would discuss the issues: the reasons for the assassination, the behaviour of the crowd. Both the activity and the discussion should be fun and arouse enthusiasm; but practical dramatic activities must be closely geared to the language, characters and themes of the play.
(c) Written Work. Possible tasks:
1 You are a fourteen-year-old in ancient Rome on the Ides of March, 44 BC. Describe everything you see and hear, and offer your own comments on what you think is happening. You will not have had access to the Senate House, so the events will be only known to you on the basis of rumour as senators are seen running out of the building. Your account could be in the form of a letter home.
2 *Knowledge about Language. Rhetoric:* Find out how this word has been used over the centuries. How do we use the term today? Examine the use of rhetorical devices in *Julius Caesar,* and consider why the use of rhetoric is so dramatically important in the play. Discussion could lead to consideration of many features in the Programmes of Study that deal with knowledge about language.

Romeo and Juliet
General comments on *Julius Caesar* are again relevant here.
(a) An Activity. Pupils in groups would prepare and take part in a dramatic presentation of the opening brawl, or the killing of Mercutio, or Capulet's angry words to Juliet in Act 3, Scene 5.

(b) Discussion. Discuss who is responsible for the deaths of Romeo and Juliet.

(c) Written Work. Imagine you were a Capulet or a Montague when Mercutio is killed. Describe the scene precisely, and then discuss who was to blame.

(d) Knowledge about Language. Oxymoron: Look up this word in a dictionary. Explain why oxymoron is such an important figure of speech in the play. Find examples in the speeches of Romeo and Juliet (Act 1, Scene 1, Romeo on 'loving hate'). Discuss other figures of speech, vocabulary, verse form, etc, and show how they convey meaning.

16 *An Assignment on Poetry.* Make your own anthology of about 16 poems on some important theme: war, the countryside, adventure, love, etc. Your anthology should include some pre-1900 English verse and some poems in English from other cultures.

Activity. Read two or three poems aloud to the class.

Discussion. Explain to the class why you have chosen the poems, and answer questions about why the poems interest you.

Written Work and Knowledge about Language. Compare and contrast the various ways your chosen poems treat the central theme. Examine how figures of speech, rhythm, rhyme, vocabulary, imagery, etc, contribute to the meaning and effectiveness of the poems.

17 *An Assignment on Fiction.* The teacher would choose two novels, one classic pre-1900 English novel and one twentieth-century novel.

Activities would include dramatisations of a scene followed by discussion of major issues.

Written Work would include an examination of the different treatment of major themes in the two novels, and the different uses of language. The differences between spoken and written forms of speech could be discussed.

18 *An Assignment on Non-literary and Media Texts.* Choose several versions of an important contemporary event: quality and popular newspaper accounts, radio coverage or a television news item or documentary. Describe and evaluate the use of language and the choice of material.

Activity. Compose your own radio news coverage of the event, specifying which channel you have prepared it for, and read this to the class.

Discussion could examine the various kinds of persuasive devices used in each medium.

Conclusion

19 The above notes are only suggestions. In practice, sample papers and assignments would have to be vetted with care, and there would have to be properly conducted pilot tests. After years of assessing GCSE coursework, examination agencies have gained lots of experience of how to assess assignments of the kind described above. Their advice to teachers would be based on professional understanding of the many complex issues involved in successful assessment of standards in English.

Reception of the NUT model

On 11 June 1993 the *TES* printed versions of the Patten tests side by side with mine. In the press release, Doug McAvoy, NUT General Secretary, wrote:

> The Government insists only its tests are worthwhile. It is wrong. Professor Brian Cox has produced a model which would meet the needs of pupils, parents and teachers and which would not be labelled educationally unsound. It happily brings together the demands of teacher assessment and formalised tests to provide more useful information than could ever be provided by the Government's tests.

What is so tragic about the events after 1991 when Kenneth Clarke sacked the professionals is that if the Cox curriculum had been left alone, only gradually improved by research in classroom practice, and assessment had been left with professionals and teachers, a great educational advance would have taken place. A final irony is that the policies of Kenneth Clarke and John Patten ended by losing the Conservatives thousands of votes. If National Curriculum English had been properly managed they could have claimed the credit. I hope my NUT model indicates how easily an enlightened policy of assessment could have been implemented if it had not been opposed by arrogance and dogmatism.

Unfortunately the publication of my NUT document did not convert the right wing. The tests in 1994 showed some improvements, but in February 1995 unrest was provoked unnecessarily once again by the Government when Sir Ron Dearing recommended that coursework for GCSE English should be increased from 40 to 50 per cent. This advice was rejected by the Government, presumably by the Prime Minister himself. He seems unwilling to understand the advantages of coursework for GCSE and the urgent need to arouse the enthusiasm of teachers for whatever assessment system is put in place. This decision about GCSE provides one further example of how politicians have damaged educational standards by blindly rejecting professional advice.

Media coverage

During all this debate I had been working with teachers, particularly the courageous and energetic Bethan Marshall of King's College, London, to gain maximum publicity for our case. I appeared on *Newsnight* and the national news, as well as on numerous radio programmes. My greatest success was on 28 February 1993 when I was allowed to give a 26 minute speech in the *Opinions* series straight into camera at 8 pm on Sunday evening on Channel 4. An abridged version was printed the next day in *The Times*. I do not think I normally perform particularly well on television; on this occasion I wrote my speech in advance, and used an autocue for the first time. To my surprise and delight I found this easy to manage. I knew the rhythms of my own speech, and found it easy to provide appropriate intonation and emphasis.

I began and ended with an account of a teacher at a meeting I addressed in Cheltenham who wept when she explained to me how the Key Stage 3 plans for assessment were ruining her teaching, the service she loved to offer to her pupils. I particularly drew attention to the low morale of the teaching profession:

> I'm outraged by the way the Government is attacking our teachers. They are overworked, underpaid and under great stress as the Government introduces more and more major changes in policy, and more and more nannying paperwork. We need to encourage teachers, to respect their expertise, and to leave the teaching of English in their hands.

With 26 minutes at my disposal I was able to marshal the main arguments against both the revised English curriculum and testing arrangements. I named names, as in this book. Afterwards I discovered that the video machine had considerably increased the impact of my speech. Many teachers videoed the talk so they could watch it later. The film was shown by heads to school governors, and excerpts were used at conferences.

This success helped the campaign, but I was already worried that the boycott was drawing media attention away from the revised English curriculum. On 15 April John Wilks, chair of LATE, commented:

> Once again John Patten has got it spectacularly wrong. He has failed to realise that it is the SATs that need to be changed, not the curriculum. His new National Curriculum for English will not recognise or properly assess the full range of pupils' achievements in English and will condemn the majority of pupils to failure. If these changes are rushed through, schools will be faced with yet more chaos and disruption. (LATE press release)

Unfortunately these arguments were not given the attention they deserved, as in June the media concentrated on stories from schools where the boycott was taking place.

Resignations

Meanwhile great changes were taking place among the players who had dominated NCC and SEAC since 1991. When in April it was announced that NCC and SEAC were to be amalgamated into SCAA, David Pascall was disappointed not to be offered the position of chairman. Conservative ministers had realised that the activities of NCC and SEAC were losing votes, and that the campaign by teachers and parents was popular. The new chair was the diplomatic, astute Sir Ron Dearing, who immediately began to consult teachers. Lord Griffiths, a highly intelligent man who had begun to realise the strength of his opponents' case, disappeared from the scene, and in educational circles has not been seen since. And on 5 May Dr John Marenbon resigned from SEAC.

Marenbon's reasons for resigning (his letter of resignation to the Secretary of State was printed on 7 May 1993 in the *TES*) bring together arguments I have described in this chapter. The immediate reason was that he believed that Paper 2 for the Key Stage 3 tests (tests of prior reading of the set anthology and the Shakespeare texts) was 'inadequate and unfair'. He had requested that this paper be postponed and carefully rewritten, but his advice had been rejected by Lord Griffiths. At this time it became clear that the right-wingers were beginning to fall out with each other, and that some, like Marenbon, were not unresponsive to the torrent of criticism from teachers.

Marenbon explained that the underlying reason for his resignation was '*the impossibility both of the timetable and the model of curriculum and assessment to which SEAC had to work.'* He wrote: '*(SEAC) was required to assess by short written tests, but these tests had to conform to the requirements of a curriculum devised with continuous assessment in mind...'*. The downgrading of course assessment lies at the heart of the problems with testing of the National Curriculum. The determination of Lord Griffiths to impose pencil-and-paper tests was a major influence on the decision in 1992 to rewrite the English curriculum. English teaching was to be dominated by the needs of assessment. The re-introduction of a large element of course assessment, as in my pilot Key Stage 3 tests for the NUT, is essential if the English National Curriculum is not to cause untold damage to standards in schools.

Dearing Diplomacy

Dearing's task

Sir Ron Dearing was appointed by John Patten to the post of chairman of SEAC and NCC on 19 April 1993. These bodies were formally replaced by the School Curriculum and Assessment Authority (SCAA) in October 1993 with Sir Ron as the new chairman. He was asked to conduct a review of the manageability of the National Curriculum and the testing system. He was given four specific tasks:

- ◆ to examine the scope for slimming down the curriculum;
- ◆ to look at the ten-level scale for children's attainments;
- ◆ to consider how the testing arrangements could be simplified;
- ◆ to look at ways of improving the central arrangements for administration of these.

He was asked to present an interim report by the end of July 1993.

John Patten appointed Sir Ron Dearing in the hope that he would extricate the Government from the shambles created by NCC and SEAC which had culminated in the Key Stage 3 boycott. The decision to award the top position to Sir Ron and not to David Pascall, who believed it had been promised to him, represented a major triumph for the teachers' campaign.

Sir Ron had achieved fame mainly for his success at the age of 49 when he took over the role of Post Office chairman. He succeeded by learning the Post Office culture, and by responding to employees' concerns before he embarked on programmes of reform. Brought up in Hull, he left school at 16, but after national service with the RAF took an economics degree at Hull University. He moved up to the civil service administrative ranks at the age of 24 by open examination. For the next 25 years he worked as a civil servant, eventually becoming a ministerial policy adviser. He had worked with both Tony Benn and Sir Keith Joseph. Before his appointment by John Patten he had served as chair of the Higher Education Funding Council, so, in his own words, he did not come to his new post in education with 'an empty head'. He had successfully merged the polytechnics' and universities' funding councils into a single body without causing too many waves.

In an interview with Colin Hughes of the *Independent* (22 April 1993) he said:

> I learnt the great value of extensive consultation before taking decisions in higher education. The obvious route was rarely the shortest route to get there.

In an interview with Clare Dean in the *TES* (28 May 1993) five weeks later he said:

> It is so tempting at the end of the first week, the end of the second week of this review to think 'ah... this is the answer'. But every week that goes by, you learn that it is more difficult than you thought.'

Not surprisingly his appointment was welcomed by teachers with some enthusiasm. After John Patten's own appointment as Education Secretary in 1992 he had put himself into a state of purdah, not attending annual meetings of teachers' organisations, and not talking and listening to teachers. Civil servants who offered him good advice were removed. His handling of the Key Stage 3 crisis revealed again and again that he had no feeling for the genuine nature of teachers' concerns. He and his Minister of State, Baroness Blatch, had listened only to the Centre for Policy Studies and other right-wing groups.

Sir Ron understood the crucial business principle (in his mid-thirties he had spent a year at the London Business School) that employees will work hard and efficiently only if they believe in the quality of the product. He also understood that those who know most about the product are the people involved in the day-to-day activities involved in its production. When I chaired the National Curriculum English Working Group these principles were always central to my thinking. If the teachers turned out to be unsympathetic to our recommendations, our plans would never be properly implemented. In chapter 4 I quoted the NUT statement of 1992 that teachers felt that the English curriculum was their possession; they enjoyed a sense of ownership. The decision of David Pascall, Lord Griffiths and their supporters to confront the teachers head on, to create a workforce which did not believe in the quality of the new curriculum and the assessment process, was always certain to cause confusion.

Immediately he was appointed, Sir Ron, a shrewd, apolitical team-work man, met the leaders of the six main teacher unions. In May and June he initiated a series of ten regional meetings each attended by about fifty experienced primary and secondary school teachers at which his goodwill and ability to listen were very much welcomed. Questionnaires were sent to a substantial number of schools. He immediately grasped that the burden of assessment on teachers was absurd. To Clare Dean he said:

> When you hear a class teacher with 35 Key Stage 1 children just coming up to the age of seven saying you have to complete 10,391 standard assessments, you realise what is involved.
> I get the feeling that it is not just what is on the table that is the workload problem but it is the whole business of ever-changing.
> I have heard primary teachers at Key Stage 1 more than once say it's heavy, it's very demanding, but if you leave us alone we will get on top of it rather than face more change.

He refuted claims that the Government intended to re-introduce selection, said he was against the old eleven-plus exams for grammar schools, and insisted he was his own man, free to write his own Report. In contrast to the attacks on the teaching profession so prevalent in previous years, he told teachers at one of his conferences in the West Midlands:

> I have one master and that is the future of our children and their life chances in the next century, not the Secretary of State nor the many interest groups, but the young people. I care as you care very much about them.

I was given a personal interview by Sir Ron on 26 July 1993, and we conversed for 75 minutes. I was impressed by his diplomatic skills and his determination to understand the issues. I later forwarded to him a copy of the letter written by forty university teachers of English attacking the revised English curriculum and printed in the *Independent* on 1 May (see p.96). My worry was that his attention would be given entirely to the problems of overload and assessment, and that the NCC changes to the English curriculum might stay unchallenged. His questions to me were courteous but sharp, as I tried to explain to him in such a short space of time the complex issues surrounding the teaching of reading, grammar, Standard English, the canon of English literature, multicultural texts and media studies. In chapter 2 I described his blunt disagreement with me concerning the importance of new attitudes to gender, and how these affect language (the likelihood today of annoying women in an audience if one uses 'he' as a generic pronoun). Throughout the interview I was conscious of the difficulty of combatting the non-professional view, fed by newspapers, that standards would inevitably rise if we returned to a simple diet of spelling tests and rote learning, with a literature curriculum based on the English classics.

Earlier in the year I had faced a similar problem when after my Channel 4 talk Lord Griffiths invited me to lunch at the Garrick in London to explain my opposition to his plans for Key Stage 3 assessments. On neither occasion did I feel confident that I had done justice to the arguments, and I felt disappointed with my performance. The problem is that most controversial issues about English teaching are not matters of 'either/or' but of 'yes, but...'. 'Spelling, punctuation, grammar are important, of course, but...'; 'It's wrong to spend too much time in the classroom talking about popular TV programmes, but...' And so on. Also to understand the problems of the typical English teacher, lay men and women probably need some knowledge of children of low ability, preferably in the classroom. I only taught in a secondary modern school for three months in 1949, but I learnt that there are no simple, easy solutions to the problems of raising low standards of achievement. Teachers of English, particularly those in our inner cities, face major problems when they try to explain their methods to middle-class people who attended independent or grammar schools. In this task the many parent-teacher meetings of 1993 achieved considerable progress.

Interim Dearing Report, July 1993

Sir Ron's Interim Report was submitted to the Secretary of State on 23 July. At that time John Patten was ill, so when the Report was published on 2 August it was accompanied by a response from Baroness Blatch, the Minister of State. She achieved some credibility, in contrast to Patten, by accepting the Report wholeheartedly and by promising to implement its proposals. Sir Ron's letter of 23 July reflected his common sense and his sensitivity to the needs of teachers. He wrote: '*the last thing our schools need is precipitate, ill-*

thought-through change.' He confessed that he had been '*deeply impressed - and at times moved - by the strong commitment of everyone concerned in education to serve our children well.'* He considered that the National Curriculum was beginning to produce results, and that teachers had welcomed its breadth and challenge: '*They want and need time to build on the commitment they have made to its implementation.'* English teachers were particularly pleased that, as he wrote to me in a letter of 2 August, '*there is a recommendation for a postponement of action on the revised English Order so that the matter can be pursued in the context of the whole curriculum.'*

The main recommendations of the Interim Dearing Report included:

◆ a slimmed down and less tightly prescribed curriculum, with some of the present content becoming optional studies;

◆ the statutory element should be higher in English (and in Wales, Welsh), maths and science because these subjects are so crucially important;

◆ a greatly reduced number of statements of attainment, thus relieving teachers of a considerable burden of recording work;

◆ the teacher should be free to use the time released (eventually 20 per cent) to serve the needs of his or her class, by introducing increased vocational studies, a foreign language earlier, etc, depending on the teaching skills available;

◆ the curriculum Orders should be slimmed down during the next eighteen months; during this period there should be a much higher level of stability, with action on English and Technology deferred so that these subjects could incorporate the new approaches to structuring the curricula;

◆ in 1994 tests should be limited to the three core subjects, and should be drastically cut. At Key Stage 2 tests would be voluntary, whereas at Key Stage 1 and Key Stage 3 they would be cut by roughly 50 per cent;

◆ through to 1996, national tests should continue to be limited to the three core subjects (plus Welsh in Wales), with a possible exception that testing might be extended in 1996 to subjects that a student chooses to discontinue at age 14, so that there would be an authoritative basis for recording attainment in the student's Record of Achievement.

Dearing proposed to publish a final Report at the end of the year. In the autumn he would consult further on whether the present ten-level scale should be retained, modified or replaced, and on the future shape of the curriculum for 14- to 16-year-olds. Administration would be made more effective and more responsive to the needs of teachers.

The initial response of teachers to this Interim Report was one of cautious optimism. Dearing's administrative skills were evident in the way the media welcomed his Report as a solution for the major problems of workload and the manageability of the curriculum. But very soon teachers realised that fundamental problems remained unaddressed. The proposals brought with them a dangerous threat to children's entitlement to a broad and balanced curriculum. The Dearing recommendation that the Programmes of Study should be divided into a statutory core and optional enrichment activities could easily result in a severe narrowing of the curriculum for many children. The statutory minimum requirements could become the *only* entitlement for pupils where the teacher was working under great pressure to achieve success in the tests. Particularly at Key Stage 1, the Dearing emphasis on basics might encourage this movement towards a narrow curriculum. Teachers had objected to the excessive workload involved in preparation and administration of the tests and in the keeping of records of levels of attainment, not to the richness and breadth of the programmes of study. And the timescale for the changes was clearly dictated by political rather than educational needs. After the controversies of 1993, many commentators argued that we needed a moratorium for several years on all testing at Key Stages 1 to 3 while a coherent policy, properly evaluated, was put into place. Research evidence needed to be assessed by professionals. Evidence from the USA suggested that a concentration on basic skills may not raise standards. The Dearing proposals addressed very astutely the Conservatives' need for a compromise and the problem of workload, but there was no evidence that the educational programme would help standards. These problems remain just as relevant in the second half of the 1990s.

Revised English Curriculum, September 1993

My worry that Dearing would not address the problem of the revised English curriculum was confirmed on 30 September 1993, when Sir Ron forwarded to the Secretary of State the NCC final recommendations for a revised English curriculum. No changes were now to take place in the curriculum used in schools until September 1995, and Sir Ron's letter to

John Patten says: '*it was clear from the consultation that there is much support amongst English teachers for features of the present curriculum and concern about aspects of the Council's first proposals.*' Unfortunately the changes introduced in the September 1993 version of the revised English curriculum of April were small. Changes to the definitions of Standard English had been introduced, and the requirement that spoken Standard English should be taught to children from ages 5 to 7 had been modified. The requirements for grammar, spelling and punctuation had been made more sensible. For example, the April version had said that six- and seven-year-old pupils' speech should include subject-verb agreement (you were, not you was) and correct forms of simple irregular verbs. However, in the new version these requirements were no longer Statements of Attainment. The Programmes of Study for Key Stage 1 simply said: '*Pupils should begin to understand the importance of appropriate subject-verb agreement and correct and consistent use of verb tenses.*' Not surprisingly, David Pascall objected strongly to what he called these watered-down proposals.

Unfortunately these small improvements left intact almost all the major flaws in the April curriculum (see chapter 5). This September document received little publicity, and I discovered in my talks to teachers that few schools had received copies. The new curriculum would be subject to the Dearing review, which would propose new working groups in 1994 to slim down the curriculum. I thought it best not to attack this curriculum too much in public in the hope that it might be quietly forgotten. I did not want to make the Conservatives feel their backs were to the wall and so force them to defend the curriculum in public so fiercely that compromises behind the scenes would be jeopardised.

The September document was particularly disgraceful in its description of the consultation exercise. Sir Ron's letter admits the truth, but the document presented the statistics in a way which blurred the almost unanimous objection of the teaching profession to the revised curriculum. Presumably the authors were anxious not to provide easy headlines to the media. The preamble confessed that '*many teachers were content with the existing Orders and did not therefore think that **any** changes were needed,*' but argued that this should be set in the context of a widespread feeling that a period of stability is required. It was implied that teachers did not want the Cox curriculum altered not because they agreed with it but because they feared further change. Teachers had been asked to say what they wished to be placed on record about the proposals. In reporting the views expressed, the document explained:

❧ (Council) quoted proportions and percentages which were those of respondents commenting on each issue. It needs to be noted, however, that many respondents do not answer each question. Thus a figure over 10 per cent is often significant in statistical terms. For example, question A1 sought views on the clarity of the new format. Sixteen per cent expressed disquiet about it, but 22 per cent chose not to comment.

Most readers were not likely to find clarity in this explanation. They would be further flummoxed when they turned to the percentages. The NCC document told us about the revised proposals for spoken Standard English:

❧ 2.13. Half the respondents were unhappy about the curriculum in AT1 (Speaking and Listening). Invariably, it was Standard English which provoked the disquiet. More specifically, 50 per cent agreed that its description needed amplification while 39 per cent thought its definition was inadequate. 25 per cent commented that Standard English should be required when appropriate, rather than irrespective of context.

2.14. There was disquiet too about the approach to defining progress in Standard English. The former chairman of NCC had, in his letter of 5 March, indicated a willingness to consider alternatives and the proposals themselves were proferred by the Secretaries of State with some reservations in this area. Consultation was consistent with that unease: 49 per cent of respondents disagreed with the proposals. The most concern was in relation to Key Stages 1 and 2: the proposed Statements of Attainment at levels 3 and 5 affected primary aged pupils and their teachers most sharply.

What does all this mean? If 49 per cent disagreed with the proposals, what happened to the other 51 per cent? Did any agree, or did all 51 per cent fail to respond to this question? It is difficult to believe that this problem of interpretation was the result of incompetence. I presume it was a deliberate attempt to obscure the fact that almost 100 per cent of respondents were opposed to many of the draft curriculum's proposals concerning spoken Standard English.

Final Dearing Report, December 1993

Sir Ron Dearing's Final Report was submitted to the Secretary of State on 20 December 1993. The key points were:

- the exisiting National Curriculum for 5 - 14-year-olds would be streamlined to release one day a week for schools to use at their own discretion;
- the reduction in curriculum content for this age group would be concentrated outside the core subjects of English, maths and science;
- for 14 - 16-year-olds, flexibility within the curriculum would be increased to allow schools to offer a wider range of academic and vocational options;
- the workload of teachers would be cut by simplification of the National Curriculum, and a reduction in the demands for testing and recording;
- the ten-level scale would be kept but simplified, and run only to the end of Key Stage 3;
- all National Curriculum subjects for 5 -14-year-olds would be reviewed in one go for September 1995;
- there would be no further change to the National Curriculum for five years after this.

The Government accepted in full all the main recommendations of the Final Dearing Report. The problem of the injustice of league tables was addressed by setting up a working group of SCAA to consider the introduction of value-added statistics for school performance, to assess whether an accurate sytem could be evolved so schools in poor neighbourhoods would be judged not on raw marks but on their ability to help children who enter with low educational standards. The ten-level scale would not only be terminated at Key Stage 3, but also the number of statements of attainment would be significantly reduced. The existing A* - G grading scale for the GCSE examination would be retained.

Immediately working groups were established to slim-down each subject. Their brief allocated to them the minimum time for this exercise, for their proposals were to be published for consultation by Easter 1994. The slimmed-down curriculum would be settled, in the light of the consultations, by the end of 1994. Schools would receive details in loose-leaf form in November 1994 and the final curriculum in January 1995. The new slimmed-down curriculum would come into force for Key Stages 1- 3 in September 1995 for the 1995-6 school year.

Slimmed-down English

A new English Working Group

The bad news for English teachers was that the new English Working Group was required to use as its model the curriculum published by NCC in September 1993. In a letter of 24 June 1994 in the *TES*, Pat Baldry from Essex attacked this decision as undemocratic:

❝ The subject working party for English took as the starting point the NCC consultation report (September 1993) produced after last year's consultation process. In doing this, teachers' support for the current Order has been ignored. The new draft proposals are based, therefore, on a document that was neither circulated widely to schools, nor put before Parliament. The existing Order for English, which is the legal requirement for the content of teaching and learning of the curriculum for English, has been shuffled to one side. Why and by whom? Undoubtedly Sir Ron Dearing was under political pressure not to use the Cox curriculum as the model.

The new English working party included a strange mix of people; there were teachers of high standing in the profession such as Dr Alastair West, vice-chair of NATE and an education authority adviser in London, and John Hickman, who teaches English at Forest Gate School, London, but also traditionalists such as Professor Arthur Pollard. How would they ever agree? The Dearing Report decreed that in all advisory groups teachers and headteachers should comprise at least half the membership. The membership would include representation of the Office for Standards in Education and an assessor from the Department for Education. The work of the groups was to be overseen by a committee of SCAA, and a member of SCAA would be a member of all advisory groups.

The main weakness of the Final Dearing Report was that the time allocated for his reforms was far too short. How could this new Working Group produce a satisfactory curriculum when they would meet for only three days, and the whole process would be completed in three months? Sir Ron Dearing was right to want to remove uncertainties, but the difficulties were too great to be resolved in this hasty manner.

This problem emerged in highly controversial form as soon as the proposals for the new slimmed-down curriculum were made public. They were forwarded to John Patten on 30 March 1994 by Sir Ron Dearing, and published in May. These were for consultation, and the consultation period lasted until 29 July. The final version, as I have explained, would be in the schools in draft form in November, and the Order would be published in January 1995.

As soon as the consultation document was published, the teacher members of the English Working Group were dismayed to discover that their recommendations had been altered, they claimed, 'beyond recognition'. Chris Woodhead, SCAA's chief executive, insisted quite categorically that 'there had been no ministerial influence'. Presumably the changes were introduced by the SCAA committee set up to oversee the working groups, and endorsed by a SCAA Council meeting on 22 March 1994. In an article on 20 May in the *TES*, Alastair West asked who had tampered with the English Order. It is typical of curriculum development under NCC, SEAC and SCAA that responsibility for changes of this kind is kept secret. As I have said before, and it is a major theme of this book, this secrecy seems to me completely unacceptable in a democratic society.

In his *TES* article Alastair West described the meetings of the English working party as good-humoured, with satisfactory access to professional officers:

> But I often felt that I glimpsed the group's most prominent member only rarely. It was a figure most apparent in his/her absence. I could not discern whether it was real or fictional, single or composite, to be propitiated or challenged. In my own mind I tended to refer to this never-quite-palpable figure as Unacceptable. If it had a first name it would be Politically, although deference made first-name terms redundant.

The figure of Politically Unacceptable, West explains, emerged from the shadows and became most prominent when the group was discussing

Standard English, the literary canon and book lists, the media and the teaching of early literacy. No attempt to broaden the basis of language study or to reintroduce the phrase 'knowledge about language' stood much chance of slipping past Unacceptable. Already the work of this group was being tampered with, even before its final proposals were rewritten, presumably by SCAA.

On 13 May 1994 the *TES* published a statement by eight teachers and one education authority adviser (Alastair West) from the Working Group. They said that they welcomed the reordering and the restructuring of the Programmes of Study which now have greater clarity, coherence and consistency, and that the move to Level Descriptions (as opposed to the Statements of Attainment in the Cox curriculum) was a significant improvement which offers greater emphasis to teachers' professional judgment in assessment. But they expressed surprise that so many of the group's recommendations *'have been ignored or changed beyond recognition since our last meeting'*. In particular they explained that they were deeply concerned by the following issues:

1. We all accept the importance of pupils' access to and usage of Standard English. However, significant changes in the wording of the Programmes of Study text now give an undue and unrealistic emphasis to Standard English from the earliest years;

2. a ten-to-four majority of the working group's voting members recommended that the lists of authors at Key Stages 3 and 4 should follow the pattern of Key Stages 1 and 2 and be exemplary. We are opposed to prescription by author because that undermines teachers' professional expertise, judgment and autonomy and will do nothing to promote enthusiastic wider reading;

3. a recommendation that a paragraph be included which addressed the language needs of bilingual children, and which was welcomed by key stage groups and other subject groups, has been ignored. Why is it that our recommendation that 'the linguistic and cultural knowledge of bilingual pupils is recognised and used when developing their competence in English' now only applies to pupils who are bilingual in Welsh?;

4. we are aware that these draft English proposals make recommendations about how pupils should be educated in the year 2000. We therefore regret there is so little reference to the reading, study and making of media texts. Nor do they sufficiently acknowledge and encourage the use of information technology within English;

5. we are aware that the document recommends a variety of approaches to the teaching of early literacy. However, we are concerned by matters of emphasis and balance between these approaches.

In his *TES* article Alastair West gave some specific examples of the alterations. In the following sentences for Key Stage 1 the sections in brackets were deleted by SCAA:

♦ '*Pupils* (may be speakers of more than one variety of English and) *should develop confidence in their ability to adapt what they say to their listeners and the circumstances.*'

♦ '*Pupils' understanding of English* (both Standard and other varieties) *should be enhanced through their reading.*'

In Key Stage 2 the requirement to '*consider some of the differences in vocabulary and grammar between Standard and non-Standard varieties of English*' had been deleted. Pupils in the original version had to '*understand the importance in more formal contexts, of consistent use of verb tenses and subject-verb agreement; acceptable, standard forms of the negative; correct use of plurals and pronouns.*' This was changed to: '*learn characteristic features of Standard English, including the consistent use of verb tenses, etc.*' This kind of alteration appeared throughout.

The most obvious change was to the heading of paragraph 3 throughout the Programmes of Study. The group recommended that this should be 'Language Study and Standard English' in order to emphasise the importance of Standard English within the context of a broader programme of language study. In the final printed version the terms were reversed, and Standard English was thus given more prominence. At every Key Stage for Speaking and Listening the bullet points referring to Standard English had been moved from the bottom to the top of the lists. Were these alterations introduced at the behest of a politician or by someone who understood the difficulties of teaching and defining Standard English? We do not know. Surely whoever made these changes, particularly the deletion of the reference to bilingual pupils, should have been available to appear on a television programme such as *Newsnight* to defend them.

Criticisms of slimmed-down English

Major criticisms of this May 1994 curriculum were soon being published. There were strong objections from the teaching profession to the treatment of spoken Standard English (again), phonics and the prescribed list of books.

In an article in *The English and Media Magazine* (no.30, Summer 1994), Katharine Perera explains that the description of spoken Standard English is still either unhelpful or downright wrong in a number of places:

❝ ... core grammatical features of Standard English are said to include: 'correct and consistent use of verb tenses'. It is easy to demonstrate that Standard English does not require the consistent use of verb tenses:

> 'I *am leaving* now because I *have been waiting* since before the train *arrived* and there is no sign of the parcel that I thought John *had promised to* send.'

Here, within one standard English sentence, there are four different (italicized) tense/aspect verb forms.

In a number of places, the document uses the word 'correct' in relation to the forms of Standard English which is completely circular, and therefore vacuous - ie Standard English is correct grammar; correct grammar is Standard English.

In the introduction this explanation is given:

> 'Standard English is distinguished from other forms of English by its vocabulary and by rules and conventions of grammar, spelling and punctuation.'

As far as vocabulary is concerned, the number of non-standard words currently used in English is actually very small. It may be that the statement refers instead to the fact that the vocabulary of Standard English is very much more extensive than the vocabulary of any single non-standard variety, because it has developed to serve a wider variety of functions. As for the characterisation of the grammar of Standard English, the phrase 'conventions of grammar' which is used in the introduction is more helpful and more accurate than the superficially appealing phrase 'grammatically correct expression' which features in the Programmes of Study. Admittedly, the better characterisation skates over the difficult issue of how, and by whom, the conventions come to be agreed but at least it is on the right lines.

Spoken Standard English was still to be introduced at an inappropriately early age. The Programme of Study for 'Speaking and Listening' at Key Stage 1 said:

❝ Pupils should be introduced with appropriate sensitivity to the importance of Standard English. Pupils should consider their own speech and how they communicate with others, particularly in more formal situations or with unfamiliar adults.

This is too early, for reasons I have explained before (page 88).

In a *TES* article of 17 June 1994, Michael Rosen enjoyed himself by pointing out that whereas by level 5 '*commas... are usually used accurately*', Sir Ron and John Patten used them differently. Do you put a comma after 'Dear Ron' or after 'Yours sincerely'? Usage varies.

Many teachers objected to the excessive emphasis on phonics in the teaching of reading. In the 1989 English curriculum the statements of attainment for 'Reading' for level 2 (5 - 7-year-olds) specified: '*Use picture and context cues, words recognised on sight and phonic cues in reading.*' The Programme of Study for Key Stage 1 said:

❝ Through the Programmes of Study for 'Reading' pupils should be guided so as to:
(a) appreciate the significance of print and the fact that pictures and other visual media can also convey meaning, *eg road signs, logos*;
(b) build up, in the context of their reading, a vocabulary of words recognised on sight;
(c) use the available cues, such as pictures, context, phonic cues, word shapes and meaning of a passage to decipher new words.

These are just a few examples from the detailed coverage in the 1989 curriculum. In the May 1994 slimmed-down curriculum the Programmes of Study for 'Reading' included a description of 'phonic knowledge' and the opportunities which should be made available for children aged 5 to 7:

❝ Phonic knowledge focuses on the relationships between print symbols and sound patterns. They should be made aware of the sounds of the spoken language and taught how symbols correspond to those sounds. Opportunities should be given for:
◆ listening to sounds in oral language to develop phonological awareness;
◆ recognising alliteration, sound patterns and rhyme and relating those to patterns in letters;
◆ considering syllables in longer words;
◆ identifying initial and final sounds in words, including sounds with rhyme;

◆ identifying and using a comprehensive range of letters and sounds (including combinations of letters, blends and digraphs), and paying specific attention to their use in the formation of words;

◆ recognising inconsistencies in phonic patterns;

◆ recognising that some letters do not produce a sound themselves but influence the sound of others, *eg final 'e', soft 'c'.*

These proposals provoked considerable argument. In *The English and Media Magazine* (no. 30, Summer 1994) Graham Frater wrote about the proposals for early reading:

❦ The Programmes of Study give prominence to phonic and graphical strategies, whilst context and meaning, as presented in this part of the document, are under-emphasised and ancillary. What is less clear is how this phonic dogma is intended to be turned into practice. Brave teachers, heeding the higher necessity to differentiate their teaching according to pupils' individual needs, will be unfazed in their own classrooms. Moreover, the level descriptions, which carry no such dogma, will support them in taking a more inclusive, balanced and pragmatic line. There is also a good deal of macho play with grammar in the programmes which is absent from the level descriptions.

A lack of recognition for the communicative purposes and social contexts of language use is to be found in AT3, Writing: there are many references to a range of genres, but few to the readerships or purposes to which the genres should be addressed. Good teachers will make up these deficiencies. It is always easier to compensate for curricular sins of omission than those of commission, but the omissions are of opportunities to raise standards in a systematic and nationwide fashion. Other omissions include a clear place for IT in the English curriculum; this is a pity since English often provided recognisably purposeful contexts for using IT. Drama is referred to but is not secure in the new document. And Media Education, which is neatly alluded to in the Programmes of Study, does not feature significantly in the new level descriptions, which must be seen as the acid tests.

Annabelle Dixon, a member of the Key Stage 1 advisory group, wrote in the *TES* (17 June 1994):

❦ Teachers want the children in their care to become fluent and competent writers and readers. What drives them to despair at present is the idea that in order to be able to prove such competence in public tests, children as young as five will have to undergo the drill of phonics such as 'the relationship between root words such as magic and magician', and also learn to 'recognise inconsistencies in phonic patterns.' Supposedly you first teach the children a rule and then confuse them by pointing out the exceptions.... The amount and nature of the phonic and spelling skills suggested as suitable for Key Stage 1 mean that there will be no time for anything else. Most important of all, it will reduce the time children will have to read and be heard read. There are a minimum number of spelling and phonic skills that children need at this age to be useful, and better that they learn these well than be overloaded by work more suited to older children.

This article was followed by discussion which emphasised the importance of phonics in the teaching of reading. My main point about the teaching of reading is that professional disagreements cannot be sorted out by a parliamentary Order. Children need different strategies to help them to read. New research may change the emphasis; teaching methods should not be prescribed by parliament.

There was still strong opposition to the lists of prescribed authors. Beverly Anderson wrote in the *TES* (3 June):

❝ Nowhere is it suggested that English-speaking students be made aware of texts in other languages, nor that they appreciate bilingualism. There is no hint that the English we now read, write, hear and speak also belongs to the Welsh, Scots, Irish, Australians, Indians and Jamaicans, to name but a few.

In her *TES* article Annabelle Dixon summed up the views of many teachers. She said that the new slimline curriculum is:

❝ one of culpable ignorance, combined with a wilfulness based on prejudice - why else the bias against bilingualism? ... There is no evidence that the authors are familiar with the realities of teaching young children from other than literate middle-class families.

And so another consultation exercise began. But for some time opposition to John Patten had united parents and the teaching profession. On 5 September 1993 the *Observer* printed a survey of over 1,000 parents, school governors, teachers, academics and others in education who agreed in voting John Patten the worst Education Secretary of the past decade. He was described as 'ignorant' and 'insolent'. In the summer of 1994 the Prime Minister at last bowed to pressure and sacked him. He was replaced by Gillian Shephard, who, like Sir Ron Dearing, immediately started talking to teachers. In the *Observer* survey interviewees were asked: '*If you were made Education*

Secretary tomorrow, what is the first thing you would do?' A recurrent reply was: *'Absolutely nothing until I had listened to parents and professionals.'* Gillian Shephard appears to have tried to follow this advice.

9

The 1995 English Curriculum: Basics without Vision

At last, a response to teachers' views!

The final slimmed-down curriculum arrived in schools in January 1995. It was surprising at first sight, in two respects. It was much shorter than the May 1994 version and had been trimmed down to a brief summary of basics. Second, on this occasion notice had been taken of the consultation with teachers, and major concessions had been introduced. Presumably, in contrast to John Patten, Gillian Shephard was willing behind the scenes to take account of professional advice.

In an article in the *TES* on 3 March 1995 the three professional officers involved in the rewriting (Sue Brindley, Sue Horner and Janet White) said that the consultation gave very clear messages (8,000 of them). Concerns had been expressed about the under-emphasis on information technology, media and drama, and so these were strengthened. Other improvements are discussed below. The general comments of the three professional officers are discussed in my Conclusion. These changes provide clear evidence that the previous consultation process of 1993 by and large ignored the views of those consulted: they cannot have been so very different in 1993. The article by the professional officers shows that they had read the articles I quoted in my previous chapter, and that under the rule of Gillian Shephard, not John Patten, they had been allowed to make some appropriate changes.

When the new curriculum was sent out in loose-leaf form in November 1994 it provoked little public discussion. *Newsnight* on BBC 2 hosted a debate between Bethan Marshall and Nicholas Tate, but otherwise this strange, abbreviated document was received by the media in almost total silence. The English curriculum appeared to have stopped providing material for sensational stories.

The final version of 1995 confirms the earlier decision to incorporate Spelling and Handwriting into the attainment target for 'Writing'. As in the consultation document, the old Statements of Attainment are replaced by 'Level Descriptions'. These are very general, and so SCAA intends to publish examples of pupils' work that relates to the different levels. The Programmes of Study are now the basis for what is to be taught. The Level Descriptions - one for each attainment target at each level - are aids to help teachers judge broadly which level of attainment fits each child. Because the ten-level scale no longer applies to Key Stage 4, it has become an *eight*-level scale, with an extra category for 'exceptional performance'. The Government's decision not to continue funding moderation of teachers' own assessments suggests that the main emphasis in assessment is intended to fall on the written tests. SCAA has sent a letter to schools saying that they do *not* need to keep extensive records of their assessments.

A style too abstract

The reduction in length means that we often end up with vague generalisations, cliches and platitudes. The document is inert in style and overly abstract. There is no sense of the delight and verve and energy that should characterise writings about English language and literature. It is certainly not an example of English writing which could be presented to children as a model.

The **Level Descriptions** are wooden and often gloriously imprecise. There is a lack of examples and specific detail. These generalised statements will be of little use when examiners are faced with the task of assessing levels of achievement. For example, the description of 'exceptional performance' for 'Reading' is as follows:

❡ Pupils confidently sustain their responses to a demanding range of texts, developing their ideas and referring in detail to aspects of language, structure and presentation. They make apt and careful comparison between texts, including considerations of audience, purpose and forms. They identify and analyse argument, opinion and alternative interpretations, making cross-references where appropriate.

What is meant by '*confidently sustain their responses to a demanding range of texts*'? Does one sustain a response simply by not contradicting oneself, or by not getting tired and confused? I suppose it was intended to mean '*support their responses by careful argument and precise references to the text*'. Presumably 'demanding' means for the average fourteen-year-old? Will the texts be demanding in terms of content or language? Texts which are apparently simple, such as Blake's *Songs of Innocence and Experience* or George Orwell's *Animal Farm*, are often very demanding when we try to analyse their effects and values. We need some examples for this requirement to make any sense. And what about 'confidently'? My responses to Shakespeare's *Measure for Measure*, Donne's *A Nocturnal upon St. Lucy's Day, being the Shortest Day* or T.S. Eliot's *The Waste Land* are hardly confident, although as a teacher I have read them many times. I am often bewildered and astonished by great literature, uncertain how to react. And what does 'identify' mean in the last sentence? Are pupils supposed to differentiate between argument and opinion? Does it mean pupils should describe well-known different interpretations of a literary text, such as the various explanations for Hamlet's delay? The generalisations sound grandly significant, but are just woolly. Lord Griffiths would not find it easy to translate these requirements into simple and precise pencil-and-paper tests.

This description of 'exceptional performance' should be compared with the description for level 5:

❧ Pupils show understanding of a range of texts, selecting essential points and using inference and deduction where appropriate. In their responses, they identify key features, themes and characters, and select sentences, phrases and relevant information to support their views. They retrieve and collate information from a range of sources.

This is a more satisfactory piece of prose than the description of 'exceptional performance'. It could equally be used for students for an Honours BA, or for level 8. I see no progression from this statement to the one for 'exceptional performance', except for words such as 'demanding' and 'confidently' which are imprecise and could cover a great range of abilities. It is extremely difficult (Graham Frater would say impossible) to assign the development of abilities in English language and literature to precise levels. This problem persuaded my Working Group in 1989 to repeat the same definition for levels 8, 9 and 10 for 'Reading'.

The lack of progression is seen most notably in the Level Descriptions for 'Writing'. Levels 7 and 8 say this about 'punctuation':

> *Level 7:* 'Paragraphing and correct punctuation are used to make the sequence of events or ideas coherent and clear to the reader.'
> *Level 8:* 'Writing shows a clear grasp of the use of punctuation and paragraphing.'

Why the change? There is no progression here, and it would have been more sensible to have repeated the level 7 description for level 8 if the authors had had the courage, like my Working Group, to admit that it is impossible to define progression with regard to punctuation at these levels.

The Level Description for 'Writing' at level 6 reads as follows:

❻ Pupils' writing often engages and sustains the reader's interest, showing some adaptation of style and register to different forms, including using an impersonal style where appropriate. Pupils use a range of sentence structures and varied vocabulary to create effects. Spelling is generally accurate, including that of irregular words. Handwriting is neat and legible. A range of punctuation is usually used correctly to clarify meaning, and ideas are organised in paragraphs.

Examiners are likely to vary widely in their interpretation of how far a pupil's work conforms to these requirements. The greatest writers in the world would hope to 'use a range of sentence structures and varied vocabulary to create effects.' This requirement covers an enormous range of writing. If pupils' writing 'often engages and sustains the reader's interest', does this mean that sometimes the reader's interest is not engaged, and at this level it is OK to write some dull passages?

Obviously the word 'often' has been introduced by the authors to give some semblance of progression when for higher levels it is removed. In chapter 6 I quoted Graham Frater on the 1993 curriculum, listing a series of level requirements without telling the reader their numbers, and challenging them to sort out the sequence. Here are the Level Descriptions for 'Writing' for level 8 and 'exceptional performance'. Which is which?

❻ *(a)* Pupils' writing shows the selection of specific features or expressions to convey particular effects and to interest the reader. Narrative writing shows control of characters, events and settings, and shows variety in structure. Non-fiction writing is coherent and gives clear points of view. The use of vocabulary and grammar enables fine distinctions to be made or emphasis achieved. Writing shows a clear grasp of the use of punctuation and paragraphing.

(b) Pupils' writing has shape and impact and shows control of a range of styles maintaining the interest of the reader throughout. Narratives use structure as well as vocabulary for a range of imaginative effects, and non-fiction is coherent, reasoned and persuasive. A variety of grammatical constructions and punctuation is used accurately and appropriately and with sensitivity. Paragraphs are well constructed and linked in order to clarify the organisation of the writing as a whole.

In fact *(a)* is level 8 and *(b)* is 'exceptional performance'. You might guess because the word 'sensitivity' is introduced for 'exceptional performance', but in my opinion the most difficult requirement comes under level 8: 'The use of vocabulary and grammar enables *fine* distinctions to be made or emphasis achieved (my italics)'. The use of grammar to make 'fine' distinctions is a considerable achievement. I wonder what examples the authors had in mind? The examples of pupils' work which SCAA is to publish will be crucial. This should have been done years ago, as the Cox Working Group recommended; but as every English teacher knows, the task will not be easy, and will take a great deal of time and money. Examples will often lead to disagreements between examiners, particularly as the Level Descriptions are so general.

The **Programmes of Study** also are in many instances unsatisfactory. We are told that for 'Reading' at Key Stage 1 the materials read and discussed should include '*interesting subject matter and settings, which may be related to pupils' own experience or extend beyond their knowledge of the everyday.*' This is blindingly obvious. For Key Stage 2 '*pupils working at Levels 1 and 2 should be given access to literature appropriate to their age and maturity.*' I should hope so. For 'Writing' at Key Stage 2 we are told that for language study pupils' '*interest in words should be extended by the discussion of language use and choices*'. What kind of 'use' and 'choices'? This is so vague and general as to be almost meaningless. Under 'Reading' at Key Stages 3 and 4 pupils should be given opportunities to '*appreciate the characteristics that distinguish literature of high quality*'. Critics have been arguing for centuries about what these are, and we are still uncertain. When I was fifteen years old I loved Siegfried Sassoon (*Everyone suddenly burst out singing*), John Buchan (*The Thirty-Nine Steps*) and Charles Morgan (*The Fountain*). I read passionately and insatiably, which is what every good teacher requires from a fifteen-year-old, not obeisance to established classics 'of high quality' he or she finds boring (in my case Pope's *Essay on Man* and George Eliot's *Silas Marner*). What constitutes literature of high quality is something for pupils to discuss, but there are no final answers.

The crucial weakness of the 1995 English curriculum concerns tone and emphasis. From the Cox curriculum of 1989 to this 1995 document the word 'taught' has increased considerably in number, and is spattered all over the document. Between the consultation and final versions some were removed, but not enough. There is a feeling of cold authority about many of the pronouncements. Occasional sentences have been inserted which teachers must leap upon, and use as permission for good practice. These brief flashes of illumination are balanced by long sections which make the teaching of English seem dull and mechanical. Some welcome sentences are the following:

◆ Under 'Reading' for Key Stage 1: '*The material read and discussed should be used to stimulate pupils' imagination and enthusiasm.*'

◆ Also under 'Reading' for Key Stage 1 the consultation document has been much improved. In the consultation version we read: '*Pupils should be taught to read with fluency, accuracy and understanding.*' This has now become: '*Pupils should be taught to read with fluency, accuracy, understanding and enjoyment, building on what they already know.*' Although this is much closer to good practice, this alteration shows why the whole document is so unsatisfactory in tone. The authoritarian 'taught' left over from the past sits uneasily side by side with the more enlightened 'enjoyment'. Can you really teach children to enjoy themselves? You can 'encourage' them. (I am reminded of the old joke about the teacher bashing a child and insisting: 'Who loves you? Jesus loves you.' In future teachers will have to order children to enjoy themselves.)

◆ Under 'Reading' for Key Stages 3 and 4 we have the following recommendation for the reading of Shakespeare and pre-1900 texts: '*Pupils should be encouraged to appreciate the distinctive qualities of these works through activities that emphasise the interest and pleasure of reading them, rather than necessitating a detailed, line-by-line study.*'

◆ Under 'Writing' for Key Stage 1 we have: '*Pupils should be helped to understand the value of writing as a means of remembering, communicating, organising and developing ideas and information, and as a source of enjoyment.*'

These welcome examples show that this is a document which teachers must edit for themselves, and that there are many sentences which could be used to support good practice in a school's own programmes of study.

It is good to see, for example, that the Key Skills at Key Stage 2 for 'Writing' include strong emphasis on the importance of drafting.

Concessions

The main changes from the consultation document relate to Standard English, the prescriptive lists of authors, media studies and drama, although, as I have already shown, there are a number of small drafting improvements throughout.

Standard English

The references to Standard English have been reduced in number, after over half the teachers consulted objected to the way this was treated in the consultation document. The inaccurate and contentious definitions criticised by Katharine Perera have been almost entirely deleted.

The General Requirement for English: Key Stages 1 - 4 now says in the first section that '*to develop effective speaking and listening pupils should be taught to use the vocabulary and grammar of Standard English.*' In the second section a general statement on Standard English and dialects reads:

In order to participate confidently in public, cultural and working life, pupils need to be able to speak, write and read Standard English fluently and accurately. All pupils are therefore entitled to the full range of opportunities necessary to enable them to develop competence in Standard English. The richness of dialects and other languages can make an important contribution to pupils' knowledge and understanding of Standard English. Where appropriate, pupils should be encouraged to make use of their understanding and skills in other languages when learning English.

This recognition of the value of the other languages spoken by bilingual children is very welcome, and one wonders who prevented such sensible words from being included in previous drafts. This is followed by a third section on Wales which begins: '*In Wales, the linguistic and cultural knowledge of Welsh-speaking pupils should be recognised and used when developing their competence in English.*' Members of the Working Group wanted this firm reference to 'linguistic and cultural knowledge' to be applied to all bilingual children, but their recommendation was deleted by SCAA Council. The fourth section reads:

❧ Pupils should be given opportunities to develop their understanding and use of Standard English and to recognise that:

◆ Standard English is distinguished from other forms of English by its vocabulary, and by rules and conventions of grammar, spelling and punctuation;

◆ the grammatical features that distinguish Standard English include how pronouns, adverbs and adjectives should be used and how negatives, questions and verb tenses should be formed; such features are present in both the spoken and written forms, except where non-standard forms are used for effect or technical reasons;

◆ differences between the spoken and written forms relate to the spontaneity of speech and to its function in conversation, whereas writing is more permanent, often carefully crafted, and less dependent on immediate responses;

◆ spoken Standard English is not the same as Received Pronunciation and can be expressed in a variety of accents.

The entitlement of all children to speak and write Standard English is affirmed, as in the Cox curriculum. But when this is read carefully it turns out to mean not much more than that Standard English is not the same as dialects. Presumably members of SCAA insisted on a statement of some length on Standard English, and we are left with these very general remarks. Katharine Perera's letter in chapter 4 provides the kind of material teachers need if they are to introduce their pupils sensibly to Standard English. They might also consult the LINC publications, and the material in *Cox on Cox* on Standard English.

All the Programmes of Study include a section on 'Standard English and Language Study'. (The reversal of the order of the heading - Standard English put first - to which Alastair West objected is retained.) Under this heading in 'Speaking and Listening' for Key Stage 1 this is written:

❧ Pupils should be introduced with appropriate sensitivity to the importance of Standard English. Pupils should be given opportunities to consider their own speech and how they communicate with others, particularly in more formal situations or with unfamiliar adults. Pupils should be encouraged to develop confidence in their ability to adapt what they say to their listeners and to the circumstances, beginning to recognise how language differs, eg the vocabulary of Standard English and that of dialects, how their choice of language varies in different situations. They should be introduced to some of the features that distinguish Standard English, including subject-verb agreement and the use of the verb 'to be' in past and present tenses. Pupils may speak in different accents, but they should be taught to speak with clear diction and appropriate intonation.

This balks at saying directly that children at Key Syage 1 who speak dialect at home should be made to start using Standard English in the classroom. It is typical of the lack of frankness in the document that it leaves the phrase '*confidence in their ability to adapt*' unrelated to a specific context. Presumably this allows teachers of children who speak dialect to introduce them at Key Stage 1 to some knowledge about language without actually forcing them to change their speech if they refuse to do so. How these requirements are introduced into the classroom must depend on the individual teacher. I am unhappy about the requirement under 'Speaking and Listening' that pupils should be introduced to features of Standard English such as '*subject-verb agreement and the use of the verb 'to be' in past and present tenses.*' How will this be done? This requirement shows little understanding of the realities of speech development. If it is tested it could lead to some very boring exercises.

Under the heading 'Standard English and Language Study' in 'Speaking and Listening' for Key Stage 2, the Programme of Study reads:

❝ Pupils' appreciation and use of Standard English should be developed by involvement with others in activities that, through their content and purpose, demand the range of grammatical constructions and vocabulary characteristic of spoken Standard English. They should be taught to speak with clear diction and appropriate intonation. Pupils should be taught how formal contexts require particular choices of vocabulary and greater precision in language structures. They should also be given opportunities to develop their understanding of the similarities and differences between the written and spoken forms of Standard English, and to investigate how language varies according to context and purpose and between standard and dialect forms.

The word 'use' appears in the first sentence. This requirement will be very difficult to implement in working-class schools. The concluding sentences about knowledge about language are acceptable, but the implicit view that children who speak dialect will be able at the top of the primary school to develop in role play or other dramatic activities a fluency in Standard English is unrealistic. Opportunities through role play may be offered, but anyone who has listened to the speech of children who speak dialect in the playground will recognise that for the majority of such children there can be little progress in spoken Standard English at this stage.

At least this draft allows teachers to discuss the virtues and grammar of dialects. The comparable paragraph in 'Speaking and Listening' for Key Stages 3 and 4 reads:

> Pupils should be taught to be fluent, accurate users of Standard English vocabulary and grammar, and to recognise its importance as the language of public communication. They should be taught to adapt their talk to suit the circumstances, and to be confident users of Standard English in formal and informal situations. In role-play and drama, the vocabulary, structures and tone appropriate to such contexts should be explored.

The worrying word 'taught' appears here. It suggests that teachers can force their pupils to abandon the language of the home, and be *made* to speak Standard English. I have already dealt at length in previous chapters with the difficulties this poses for the teacher. The word should be 'encouraged'. Will spoken Standard English be assessed? I suspect not.

Under the heading 'Standard English and Language Study' in 'Reading' for Key Stage 1, the Programme of Study is reduced to the following:

> Pupils should be given opportunities to consider the characteristics and features of different kinds of texts, *eg beginnings and ending in stories*. They should be taught to use their knowledge about language gained from reading, to develop their understanding of Standard English.

What is covered by '*the characteristics and features of different kinds of texts*'? The example does not give much help. Teachers are free to interpret this huge generalisation as they wish. For Key Stage 2 this short paragraph is changed to the following:

> Pupils should be introduced to the organisational, structural and presentational features of different types of text, and to some of the appropriate terms to enable them to discuss the texts they read, eg *author, setting, plot, format*. They should be encouraged to use their knowledge gained from reading to develop their understanding of the structure, vocabulary and grammar of Standard English.

At Key Stage 1 pupils 'should be taught to use their knowledge' while at Key Stage 2 they 'should be encouraged'. Why are young children 'taught' and children at the top end of primary school 'encouraged'? This is another piece of sloppy drafting, which presumably once again illustrates the disagreement between the SCAA right-wingers and the professional officers. At Key Stage 1 pupils are asked '*to develop their understanding of Standard English*', while at Key Stage 2 this becomes '*their understanding of the structure, vocabulary and grammar of Standard English*'. Does the longer description at Key Stage 2 mean children at Key Stage 1 will not be concerned with '*structure, vocabulary and grammar*'? What will they be doing? The attempt to introduce a spurious idea of progression produces many imprecisions of this kind. The impression from these sentences is that this somewhat reductive view of reading has been manipulated rather crudely to introduce references to Standard English.

Under 'Reading' for Key Stages 3 and 4 the reference to Standard English is reduced to:

❧ Pupils should be taught [not encouraged!] to consider features of the vocabulary and grammar of Standard English that are found in different types of text, *eg technical terms in reports, rhetorical devices in speeches.*

This is a huge requirement. It is open to a variety of teaching strategies, and schools will have to decide themselves what programmes of study are appropriate.

Under 'Standard English and Language Study' in 'Writing' for Key Stage 1 the Programme of Study reads:

❧ Pupils should be introduced to the vocabulary, grammar and structures of written Standard English, including subject-verb agreement, and the use of the verb 'to be' in past and present tenses.

This brings out a major flaw in the document: it includes leftovers from past versions which sit uneasily in this new context. What does 'introduced' mean? Almost all the books they read will be in Standard English. Some teachers might think this meant exercises in simple grammar, while others might be happy to discuss such matters in the context of the children's own reading and writing. It is typical of the document that such important but difficult issues are avoided. Teachers who read this can quietly go their own way.

For Key Stage 2 we are told that:

❧ Pupils should be given opportunities to reflect on their use of language, beginning to differentiate between spoken and written forms. They should be given opportunities to consider how written Standard English varies in degrees of formality.

Without any examples I find this uncertain in meaning. Does it mean they should understand the difference between formal prose and narrative with dialogue? Will they be comparing a sermon, for example, with a piece of journalism?

For Key Stages 3 and 4 we are told:

> Pupils should be encouraged to be confident in the use of formal and informal written Standard English, using the grammatical, lexical and orthographic features of Standard English, except where non-standard forms are required for effect or technical reasons.

What is 'informal written Standard English'? Does it mean dialogue, or the style, for example, of D.H. Lawrence's letters? This needs explanation, and there are many possibilities.

The Level Descriptions include no references to Standard English for 'Reading' or 'Writing'. Standard English is crucial for 'Writing', and this is a major error. The following statements appear under 'Speaking and Listening':

Level 3: '*They are beginning to be aware of Standard English and when it is used.*'
Level 4: '*They use appropriately some of the features of Standard English vocabulary and grammar.*'
Level 5: '*They begin to use Standard English in formal situations.*'
Level 6: '*They are usually fluent in their use of Standard English in formal situations.*'
Level 7: '*They show confident use of Standard English in situations that require it.*'
Level 8: '*They show confident use of Standard English in a range of situations, adapting as necessary.*'
Exceptional performance: '*They show assured and fluent use of Standard English in a range of situations and for a variety of purposes.*'

My granddaughter, aged 6, is certainly up to level 8 on this scale! All her family speak Standard English, so she has no problem. She certainly adapts her speech according to whether she is speaking rudely to her younger brother or politely to me. This is all very silly, and the curse of David Pascall hovers over these Level Descriptions. If this is to be tested, many intelligent working-class children who speak vividly and forcibly will have difficulty in proceeding beyond level 6, while a dull middle-class child will easily manage an exceptional performance. The objections I have already discussed to the allocation of spoken Standard English to levels still apply. These requirements reflect the need of politicians at

Tory Party conferences to make attacks on yob speak to please the audience. They are not helpful for real children in the classroom.

Knowledge about language and grammar

In this slimmed-down curriculum the references to knowledge about language and grammar have become sporadic and disorganised. Progression from one level of understanding to the next is usually unclear, and attempts to add new activities for the more advanced key stages often only include those which are normal at Key Stage 1, although not mentioned for Key Stage 1 here.

I have already dealt with the elements of knowledge about language which appear in the references to Standard English. The following is a summary of the other main references. By and large the innovative proposals for knowledge about language in the Cox curriculum are replaced by a study of vocabulary and grammar which is likely to be tedious and counter-productive.

Speaking and Listening. The section on 'Standard English and Language Study' for Key Stage 1 includes some proposals about vocabulary:

> Pupils' vocabulary should be extended through activities that encourage their interest in words, including exploration and discussion of:
> ◆ the meanings of words and their use and interpretation in different contexts;
> ◆ words with similar and opposite meanings;
> ◆ word games;
> ◆ words associated with specific occasions, *eg greetings, celebrations*;
> ◆ characteristic language in storytelling, *eg 'Once upon a time'* .

This material on vocabulary shows how the desire to slim down the curriculum ends up with the banal. Do we need a national curriculum to repeat such obvious teaching strategies? There is nothing new or exciting here. At Key Stage 2 this becomes:

> Pupils should be taught to use an increasingly varied vocabulary. The range of pupils' vocabulary should be extended and enriched through activities that focus on words and their meanings, including:
> ◆ discussion of more imaginative and adventurous choices of words;
> ◆ consideration of groups of words, *eg word families, the range of words relevant to a topic*;
> ◆ language used in drama, role-play and word games.

Only at Key Stages 3 and 4 are pupils allowed a more adventurous approach to language study:

❧ Pupils should be given opportunities to consider the development of English, including:
   ◆ how usage, words and meanings change over time;
   ◆ how words and parts of words are borrowed from other languages;
   ◆ the coinage of new words and the origins of existing words;
   ◆ current influences on spoken and written language;
   ◆ attitudes to language use;
   ◆ the differences between speech and writing;
   ◆ the vocabulary and grammar of Standard English and dialectical variations.

This includes some intriguing permissive generalisations. What are 'current influences on spoken and written language' and 'attitudes to language use'? A whole programme on knowledge about language could be developed under these headings. They allow teachers to initiate discussions about the social and political attitudes to language which were implied in the changes introduced into the English curriculum by David Pascall and NCC in 1993. I hope teachers will introduce children at an earlier stage to 'how usage, words and meanings change over time'; in classes with bilingual children borrowings from other languages and comparison between languages can start at a very early age.

Reading. As with 'Speaking and Listening' the main opportunities for study of language are reserved for Key Stages 3 and 4. This reads:

❧ Pupils should be taught:

   ◆ about the main characteristics of literary language, including figures of speech and sound patterning;
   ◆ to consider features of the vocabulary and grammar of Standard English that are found in different types of text, *eg technical terms in reports, rhetorical devices in speeches*;
   ◆ to analyse and evaluate the use of language in a variety of media, making comparisons where appropriate, *eg the treatment of a traditional story in a children's picture book and in its original source; a comparison of a television news bulletin with a report on the same event in a newspaper*;
   ◆ about different genres and their characteristics, including language, structure and organisational features;
   ◆ to analyse techniques, *eg the portrayal of setting and period, the weaving of parallel narratives, time shifts, the building of suspense, the use of imagery.*

Once again the list here is so general teachers can adopt all kinds of teaching strategies. Why should 'the main characteristics of literary language' be followed by special mention of 'figures of speech and sound patterning'? This is a very careless sentence.

Writing. Teachers complained that the requirements in the Level Descriptions for level 1 were too difficult. In the consultation document we had the following: '*Pupils begin to show an awareness of full stops, identifying where they are needed in their own writing.*' In the 1995 version this becomes: '*In their reading or their writing, pupils begin to show awareness of how full stops are used.*' This is a useful concession.

At Key Stage 1 the recommendations in the Programme of Study are mainly concerned with spelling, punctuation and handwriting. Knowledge about language is reduced to an interest in words and their dictionary meanings. Grammar is introduced forcefully at Key Stage 2:

> Pupils should be given opportunities to develop their understanding of the grammar of complex sentences, including clauses and phrases. They should be taught how to use paragraphs, linking sentences together coherently. They should be taught to use the standard written forms of nouns, pronouns, verbs, adjectives, adverbs, prepositions, conjunctions and verb tenses.
>
> Pupils should be taught to distinguish between words of similar meaning, to explain the meanings of words and to experiment with choices of vocabulary. Their interest in words should be extended by the discussion of language use and choices.

As I pointed out above, the last sentence could mean anything. *What* language use and *what* choices? All these requirements are typical in underemphasising the importance of meaning and communication. They encourage a concentration on language games and exercises in isolation from the pupils' use of language for real audiences.

The recommendations for Key Stage 3 and 4 are as follows:

> Pupils should be encouraged to broaden their understanding of the principles of sentence grammar and be taught to organise whole texts effectively. Pupils should be given opportunities to analyse their own writing, reflecting on the meaning and clarity of individual sentences, using appropriate terminology, and so be given opportunities to learn about:
> - discourse structure - the structure of whole texts; paragraph structure; how different types of paragraphs are formed; openings and closings in different kinds of writing;

◆ phrase, clause and sentence structure - the use of complex grammatical structures and the linking of structures through appropriate connectives; the use of main and subordinate clauses and phrases;

◆ words - components including stem, prefix, suffix, inflection; grammatical functions of nouns, verbs, adjectives, adverbs, pronouns, prepositions, conjunctions and demonstratives;

◆ punctuation - the use of the full range of punctuation marks, including full stops, question and exclamation marks, commas, semi-colons, colons, inverted commas, apostrophes, brackets, dashes and hyphens.

In a slimmed-down curriculum this detailed list is worrying. It could lead to boring grammatical exercises of no value in helping children to improve the quality of their writing. This begins by saying that 'pupils should be given opportunities to analyse their own writing', and so be given opportunities to learn about grammar. These words need to be heavily emphasised when these proposals are translated into school programmes of work. The requirements for 'Writing' often seem particularly mechanistic, and may do harm if teachers obey them too slavishly.

The Level Descriptions almost completely abandon any reference to knowledge about language. Why?

Phonics and reading

Under the heading 'Key Skills' in 'Reading' for Key Stage 1 there is this general requirement:

Pupils should be taught the alphabet, and be made aware of the sounds of spoken language in order to develop phonological awareness. They should also be taught to use various approaches to word identification and recognition, and to use their understanding of grammatical structure and the meaning of the text as a whole to make sense of print.... Within a balanced and coherent programme, pupils should be taught to use the following knowledge, understanding and skills.

The words 'various' and 'balanced' are very welcome. This balanced approach is explained under five headings: 'phonic knowledge', 'graphic knowledge', 'word recognition', 'grammatical knowledge' and 'contextual understanding'. 'Phonic knowledge' comes first, and so is given prominence. The list is almost exactly the same as in the consultation document, to which Annabelle Dixon objected in the *TES* on 17 June 1994 (see chapter 8). The one major change is that the following requirement has been deleted: opportunities should be given for '*listening to sounds in oral language to develop phonological awareness*'. This deletion is an improvement, but Annabelle Dixon's objections stand. The requirement that these young children at Key Stage 1 should be given opportunities for '*recognising inconsistencies in phonic patterns*' has not been removed. Graham Frater's criticism of the consultation document that too much prominence is given to phonic and graphical strategies, while context and meaning are underemphasised, also still stands.

The changes under 'graphic knowledge' are minimal. The example of a 'relationship between root words' in the consultation document was *magic,* and derivatives, eg *magician.* This has become 'relationships between root words and derivatives, *eg help, helpful*'. I hope this choice reflects a change of attitude among the authors at SCAA.

Under 'word recognition' the following sentence has been deleted: '*A significant marker of pupils' progress in reading in this key stage is the ability to read aloud 30 common usage words within simple, short narratives.*' This deletion presumably reflects the views of teachers during the consultation period. If this requirement had been tested it would have led to bad teaching, with children learning words out of context. The number 30 was presumably included so that simple assessment would be possible. Thank goodness this is no longer thought necessary.

While the 1995 document includes many sensible requirements for the teaching of reading, the descriptions of reading activities in the Cox Report are much more detailed and encouraging and enriching.

Prescribed lists of authors

The suggested lists of authors and books for Key Stages 1 and 2 in the May document have been deleted. Teachers can now choose books as they please. Key Stage 1 in 'Reading' begins with welcome comments on 'range':

❧ (a) Pupils should be given extensive experience of children's literature. They should read on their own, with others and to the teacher, from a range of genres that includes stories, poetry, plays and picture books. Pupils should read their own writing to the teacher and others.

(b) Pupils should be introduced to and should read information, both in print and on screen. They should be encouraged to make use of a range of sources of information, including dictionaries, IT-based reference materials, encyclopaedias and information presented in fictional form.

The reference to IT-based reference materials is welcome, and this is repeated in the later Key Stages.

For Key Stages 3 and 4 the canon of twentieth-century literature has been dropped, although the mandatory lists of pre-1900 authors are retained. Teachers still have to choose two plays by Shakespeare, two works of fiction 'of high quality' by major writers, published before 1900, and 'poems of high quality by four major poets, whose works were published before 1900'. The lists of what is called the English literary heritage are long and inclusive, and should not cause teachers much anxiety. A list of drama by major playwrights has been added. The examples given are Christopher Marlowe, J.B. Priestley, G.B. Shaw and R.B. Sheridan. It is not surprising that SCAA preferred J.B. Priestley to John Osborne or any of the more subversive post-1945 dramatists. The list is only exemplary, so teachers are not constrained. Teachers in Wales may be disappointed that their arguments for special recognition for Wales and against any prescription have been ignored.

Examples from the English heritage are now balanced by a number of significant references to texts in English from other cultures. In the 'Common Requirements' which introduce the document we are told that to develop as effective readers pupils should be taught to '*read, analyse and evaluate a wide range of texts, including literature from the English literary heritage and from other cultures and traditions.*' For Key Stage 1 'Reading' literature should include 'stories and poems from a range of cultures', and for Key Stage 2 'texts drawn from a variety of cultures and traditions' (what is the difference?). For Key Stages 3 and 4 the document says: '*Pupils should read texts from other cultures and traditions that represent their distinctive voices and forms, and offer varied perspectives and subject matter.*' The Level Descriptions mention neither the English literary heritage nor texts in English from other cultures; they simply ask for a response to 'a range of texts'. These alterations represent a success for teachers, and a defeat for the Little England mentality which is afraid of variety in the richness of our English culture.

Media studies

In an essay 'Media Studies makes the Grade' on 16 December 1994 in the *TES* Cary Bazalgette, who organised the BFI Commission of Inquiry into English, expressed delight at the changes to the May 1994 curriculum. 'The news is good,' she wrote, and she particularly welcomed the requirement in the Programmes of Study in 'Reading' for Key Stages 3 and 4:

❡ Pupils should be introduced to a wide range of media, *eg magazines, newspapers, radio, television, film.* They should be given opportunities to analyse and evaluate such material, which should be of high quality and represent a range of forms and purposes, and different structural and presentational devices.

For Cary Bazalgette this improves on the Cox curriculum, because study of the media is not just crammed into 'non-fiction', but is recognised in its own right. Substantial requirements for attention to the media also appear in the 1995 Orders for modern foreign languages. In the English Orders there are various other references which ask pupils at Key Stage 2 to listen and respond to radio and television, and at Key Stages 3 and 4 to talk about the media.

Drama

Particularly welcome is the increased emphasis on drama. Under 'Speaking and Listening' for Key Stage 2 the Programme of Study reads: '*Pupils should be given opportunities to participate in a wide range of drama activities, including improvisation, role-play, and the writing and performance of scripted drama.*' Under 'Writing' for Key Stage 2 they are encouraged to experiment with drama scripts. Under 'Speaking and Listening' for Key Stages 3 and 4 we have: '*Pupils should be given opportunities to participate in a wide range of drama activities, including role-play, and in the performance of scripted and unscripted plays.*' Although I am pleased to read this, once again the drafting is bad. Why do the requirements for Key Stage 2 include 'improvisation' while those for Key Stages 3 and 4 do not? What is the difference between '*should be encouraged to evaluate their own and others' contributions*' (Key Stage 2) and '*should be given opportunities to consider significant features of their own and others' performances*' (Key Stages 3 and 4)? Is the word 'significant' supposed to indicate some kind of progression? There are no references to media studies or dramatic activities in the Level Descriptions. Why?

This peculiar document opens doors. Most restrictions in the 1993 and 1994 drafts have been removed. What is left is often bare, boring and brief, but good teachers are allowed to develop their own initiatives.

On 23 December 1994 in the *TES* Alastair West asked for a Christmas present from Santa Claus (the Government): an increase in the proportion of coursework assessment in the new criteria for GCSE syllabuses. In January 1995 he discovered that his stocking was empty, and coursework would remain at 40 per cent, against the recommendation by Sir Ron Dearing himself that it should be 50 per cent. The problem with the vagueness and permissiveness of the 1995 English curriculum is that it could be tested in any way that SCAA thought appropriate. Will the tests be reduced to basics so that teachers forced to teach to the test will cut out many enriching activities? Will the lack of any reference to dramatic activites or media studies in the Level Descriptions prove a deliberate omission of immense significance?

What Next?

Since 1991 teachers of English have spent a great deal of time responding to absurd curriculum proposals from NCC, SEAC and SCAA. This has been a heart-breaking waste of time and money. The new 1995 curriculum allows some freedom to go back to where we left off in 1991, and to consider professional advice for improving the Cox curriculum and new initiatives for raising standards. SCAA itself must be reformed as soon as possible, and professionals enlisted with up-to-date knowledge of what is best for children and the respect of the teaching community. Non-statutory advice would help teachers to improve their programmes of study. The success of these reforms depends on sensible testing arrangements, with an increased use of course assessment so the richness of the English curriculum (drama, the craft of writing, speaking and listening, media studies, etc) should not be downgraded by the imposition of reductive tests confined to basics.

In this chapter I outline the context in which we need to develop this non-statutory advice, the problems for teachers of English, and the debates about English studies which in recent years have led to passionate interchanges in the universities. I deal quickly with a diversity of major issues; my aim is to ask questions, and to describe areas where discussions need to continue.

Reading: the social context

A friend of mine who teaches in a junior school in a depressed area found a seven-year-old boy hanging about in the toilets. When asked what he was doing the boy replied that he was hungry. My friend was mystified until further questions revealed the boy wanted to drink from the water fountain. He did not know the difference between 'hungry' and 'thirsty'.

Another teacher in the same school was taking a junior class on a guided walk. As they approached a church he shouted: 'We'll pause here.' The children went on walking. They did not know what 'pause' meant. These children were white, so there was no second language problem. Teachers of this age group know that words such as 'return' or 'consider' may not be understood, and that some young children cannot distinguish between 'over' and 'under'. A child recently said: 'She's my brother.' Another wanted an explanation of the difference between Mr and Mrs. These children probably come from homes where the parents are themselves semi-literate and often unemployed. The television usually stays on all day, and the table may never be set for a meal. Research reports constantly show that poor readers come from families where the parents have little time for conversation with their children, and, in some cases, rarely see them.

Semi-literate children will probably arrive at secondary school bearing a grudge against school because of their failure, and they provide a large percentage of the truants and misfits who create discipline problems. When they leave school they are almost unemployable except for the most menial tasks.

According to the Bullock Report of the 1970s, approximately one million adults in England had a reading age below nine, although to read even the simplest daily newspaper requires a reading age of at least thirteen. The situation must be roughly similar today. Surveys have discovered that some homes in poor areas possess no books of any kind. Teachers complain that children from such backgrounds regress during the summer holidays, for in homes where there are few books reading habits soon deteriorate.

That low standards in reading are very much influenced by social problems and lack of parental support is well-known to teachers and researchers, but usually ignored by tabloid newspapers when they produce a scare story about low standards and teacher incompetence. Their readers enjoy hearing about the failings of teachers, so these stories are regular fare. Anyone who visits schools in deprived areas knows that teachers face extraordinarily difficult problems when they try to help children who arrive at school with serious language deficiencies.

These problems have been exacerbated in the 1980s and 1990s because the Conservative Government has allowed spending on school and public library books to fall dramatically. In many schools spending in real terms on books has fallen by at least 50 per cent since the 1970s. In many primary schools children are forced to use an inadequate supply of dog-eared readers which may fall to pieces in their hands. By the mid-1980s primary schools were spending on school books at a rate only 60 per cent of the National Book League's criterion for 'reasonable' provision. Public library spending during the first five years of the Conservative's period of office fell about a quarter in real terms. Ten years later the situation is worse. In February 1995 savage cuts were announced in public library provision, including the closure of many branch libraries and major cuts in book-buying funds. The Library Association said that most library authorities were expecting cuts of at least 5 per cent in their budgets, and some over 20 per cent. These are among the major reasons for low standards in reading. Schools in middle-class areas raise considerable sums of money to help buy books. A toy fair may produce £400. A head teacher in a deprived area will be lucky to make £40 from a similar event.

Book Flood experiments in New Zealand, the United States and in the late 1970s in Bradford demonstrate the importance to schools of a supply of new books. In the Bradford experiment a few middle schools were flooded with over 5,000 children's books, while other schools with normal provision were used as a control group. A major conclusion of this research was that children in the Flood schools developed the habit of reading much more rapidly than those in normal schools. The research showed the need to allow children, particularly when parents are not well off, to take home books. This means money must be made available annually for the replacement of the inevitably lost and damaged books. The obvious corollary is that children in deprived areas must be provided with first-class facilities for reading in their schools.

Particularly frightening is the emergence of large numbers of semi-literate unemployed young people in our inner cities. Such groups are particularly susceptible to the rhetoric of demagogues. As W.H. Auden wrote: '*When words lose their meaning, physical force takes over.*'

During the last few years the gap between the educated and the uneducated, employed and unemployed, rich and poor, has widened alarmingly. The numbers of ill-educated unemployables create vast social problems, and are clearly related to the high levels of juvenile delinquency and crime. By reducing spending on school books, and, of course, more generally on education, the Government is ensuring that more money must be spent on law and order. It is a crazy sequence. I have already commented on the large sums of money wasted by the Conservative Government in its foolish attempts to revise the English curriculum. The losses incurred by all the curriculum alterations since 1991 are often said to amount to at least £650 million. It is impossible for me to calculate, but the wastage figure must be enormous when one considers the expensive publications sent to every school, the staff salaries at NCC, SEAC and SCAA, and, above all, the amount of time wasted by teachers in responding to ill-considered new initiatives.

Conservatives often accuse teachers of always reacting to low standards in education by asking for more money rather than by addressing problems created by teaching deficiencies. I have found that most teachers of English are willing to discuss new methods and to spend their evenings and weekends in preparation of new material. The failure of a certain percentage of children to reach level 2 at age seven is largely a social problem, which no new national curriculum can solve by itself. Teachers trying to introduce English in the National Curriculum have had their tasks made much more difficult because of lack of money, lack of books and teaching materials. A reformed SCAA, an independent body, ought to press the Government hard on this issue.

How to teach reading

The Programmes of Study in the Cox Report provide detailed accounts of appropriate activities for the teaching of reading. I have already quoted a few sentences in chapter 8. Crucial among them is the requirement that children should be helped to read by a variety of approaches, to '*use the available cues, such as pictures, context, phonic cues, word shapes and meaning of a passage to decipher new words.*' Such a balanced approach, as we have seen, is allowed by the 1995 curriculum. The brief descriptions of phonic and graphic knowledge are not particularly helpful, but good teachers should be able to develop programmes in accord with good practice. Phonics is an aid, a word-attack skill, to be learnt and used when appropriate, not a total scheme in itself. On 22 July 1994 Suzanne Tiburtius wrote in a letter in the *TES*:

❝ We badly need a rest from the confrontation between the 'phonics forever' brigade and the sweet but misguided optimism of those who make such assured statements as 'there is no book that a child cannot read if an adult will read it for him.'

It is a pity that those promoting what came to be known as the 'real books' theory of developing literacy did not content themselves with adding the very good ideas which they had about listening to children read and fostering a love of reading to the sum total of what has been found to improve reading standards, without rubbishing all other methods and proclaiming (another) Holy Grail.

Both the Warwick Report and HMI reports in the 1990s confirm that the majority of teachers use a variety of methods, including phonics, in the teaching of reading. It is a fallacy that all children follow the same path to literacy. Some thrive on a diet heavily dependent on teaching of phonics. Others learn to read almost effortlessly by being introduced to books they enjoy by parents or teachers. Teachers in training need to understand the variety of methods available to them, and to know how to interpret a child's errors. This kind of specialised knowledge comes from professionals, not from the brief list of approaches in the 1995 curriculum. In their article on 3 March 1995 in the *TES* the three professional officers from SCAA insist there is no implied methodology in the new curriculum document, and the revised Order is to be taught according to teachers' professional judgments.

An integrated approach brings together speaking and listening, reading and writing. For example, on 17 June 1994 in the *TES*, Geoff Barton, co-editor of *You Never Know*, an anthology of stories for reluctant readers, discussed the problem for pupils who are not attracted to independent reading, for whom social interaction, rather than solitude, is important. He recommends that such reluctant readers, who probably do not have a reading culture at home, should be given at school frequent opportunities to discuss what they have read and to make part of the reading process a social activity:

> Planning these opportunities means that we need regularly to place pupils in pairs and groups to discuss texts that they might have read in a full-class context, in groups, or at home. It means ensuring that every encounter with a book is not automatically followed by writing a review, but instead leads to a variety of activities - some spoken, some written.
>
> This is not to dispense with library lessons or private reading, but to emphasise different aspects of reading, rather than an unhelpful polarisation between the class novel and silent reading.

These are the kind of proposals which a reformed SCAA might send out to schools for discussion in the development of new Programmes of Study.

I particularly wish to emphasise the importance of knowledge about language to teachers, as well as to children. The LINC work needs to be revived and supported by the Government as soon as possible if we are to raise standards. At a professional level, there needs to be discussion of structured, integrated programmes of work for teachers and pupils which bring together speaking and listening, reading, writing and knowledge about language. These innovative proposals in the Cox curriculum need to be reconsidered, tried out in practice, and evaluated. Teachers are considerably helped in their teaching of English if they themselves understand the way language works in use, and this can only be learnt by properly organised training programmes in appropriate institutions. Teachers in training obviously need practice in the classroom, but its importance should not lead to neglect of other kinds of professional training.

The Kingman Committee (1988) recommended *'that all intending teachers of primary school children should undertake a language course in which the larger part of the time allocated to the course (ie over 50 per cent) be spent in direct tuition of knowledge about language as outlined in the model proposed in this report which is relevant to the primary school child as displayed through the attainment targets'* (6.5.). The Kingman Committee also recommended *'that all intending teachers of English in secondary schools should undertake a course which enables them to acquire, understand and make use of knowledge about language as outlined in the model proposed in this report which is relevant to the secondary school pupil as displayed through the attainment targets'* (6.6.).

The 1989 National Curriculum in English made wider demands on English teachers than had been made in the past (eg in speaking and listening, media studies and information technology). Teacher trainers need to have clear ideas about how courses can be structured for maximum benefit, to consider how much time should be spent on oral language, on the teaching of writing, on children's literature and on knowledge about language as a contribution to the teaching of reading. For example, an important aspect of children's oral language development (and of practical activities in the infant classroom) is the appreciation of phonological patterns of rhyme and alliteration. Rather than this oral/aural ability being considered by teacher-trainees in isolation, and books of rhymes and poems being treated simply as part of a children's literature course, students should simultaneously be taught how important such phonological awareness is in learning to read.

Many studies have shown that in the early stages of reading English children use a whole word rather than a letter-by-letter approach to reading. As phonological awareness relates to sounds, it is hard at first to see how it could facilitate reading if children are not using a sound-based reading strategy. The answer seems to be that some children are able to use a process of analogy when they meet new words; and they do that by relating the visual structure of a new word to the visual and phonological structure of a word they already know. So, if they can read the word *house* and they come across the word *mouse* their recognition of the letter-string *-ouse* which is shared by both words puts them in a position to exploit their implicit awareness of rhyme (a type of phonological awareness) in decoding the new word. Those children who are sensitive to rhyme do not need to identify the individual letters *-o-u-s-e* and their related sounds (and indeed they should not, since that kind of letter-by-letter sounding out will never produce -ouse) because they can treat the whole string, and its associated pronunciation, as a unit (see the writings of U. Goswami). Knowledge of this kind of research is of vital importance as teachers apply their study of phonics to classroom situations.

I give these examples to show that the teaching of reading needs trained specialists. Teachers need to study the language of early reading materials - to consider, for example, how far they should mirror children's own usage. They need to know about the difference between 'home' and 'school' language, speech and writing, dialect and Standard English. Similarly, in learning about writing, students have to learn about the English writing system, about the grammatical differences between spoken and written language, about what an alphabetical system is, how the system works, its principles and how far these are fulfilled in practice. Teachers do not need to give young children detailed information about the rules and regularities which govern the English writing system. For example, in the classroom teachers may show children irregular words in their families (*fight, night, sight; medical, medicate, medicine*). Teachers themselves need knowledge about the families and their associated reading problems (the use of 'c', for example). They need to understand how the teaching of spelling and reading are interrelated.

The slimmed-down 1995 English curriculum must not be used as a *vade mecum*, a manual regarded as giving sufficient knowledge about the teaching of reading. I have given these examples to show why knowledge about language must be restored to its rightful place in a national curriculum, why it is of great value particularly to teachers as they struggle with the language problems of little children. As I have shown, the Government's decision to cut back funding for LINC has harmed standards in the teaching of reading. New ideas need to be carefully evaluated and understood by classroom teachers.

Reading and literature

Although teachers of reading face major problems because of social deprivation and lack of resources, there is no need to be too pessimistic about standards in reading and its place in contemporary society. Last week I was travelling on the London Underground. Beside me sat a young man with an ear-ring, a tuft of orange hair and tattered jeans. He was reading Dostoevsky's *Crime and Punishment.* It is not true that young people have entirely abandoned reading for video and film. Evidence from Gallup, the polling organisation, is that more people today own encyclopaedias, dictionaries and Shakespeare plays than households in the 1950s, and that more than 60 per cent of the population claim to buy books regularly. Bookshops burgeon, and supermarkets compete to sell cut-price fiction. Figures released by the Publishers' Association in February 1995 showed that the market in books grew significantly in 1993, despite the recession, with sales, adjusted for inflation, up 5.2 per cent. In 1994 this progress was not maintained, but these figures show that there is no evidence for a decline in the habit of reading books. Books have maintained their share of spending on recreation, despite the fierce competition from videos, compact discs and computers. Britain spends an average of £43.73 per adult per year on books, compared with £39.98 in France, £30.80 in the Netherlands, £49.98 in Germany and £53.43 in the United States. In Britain public libraries are used more, with eleven loans per person on average per year, compared with fewer than two in France or Germany. Such figures, of course, hide all kinds of variables, but they do demonstrate that melodramatic stories about a huge decline in reading in Britain are untrue. They also show the great importance of public libraries in maintaining high standards.

Such figures need to be held in mind when we consider the future of the teaching of the English classics in schools. In recent months television productions have put Dickens's *Martin Chuzzlewit*, George Eliot's *Middlemarch*, and Edith Wharton's *The Buccaneers* into the best-seller lists. Teachers of English often choose their profession because of their passion for great books. For me when I was in my teens the reading of *Great Expectations* or Milton's *Il Penseroso* or Marvell's *The Garden* threw me into extraordinary states of enthusiasm and ecstasy. I chose to teach English (my father wanted me to study maths, my best subject) because of this passion. As a teacher I think of myself as the bearer of gifts; it is a privilege to share my pleasures with so many young people.

Because I want all children to have the opportunity to enjoy the classics of English literature does not mean that I support a prescribed canon of set authors. The Cox curriculum left teachers free to choose authors within a simple three-part framework: texts for study should be taken from different genres, from pre-1900 English literature, including Shakespeare, and from texts in English from other cultures. We need to return to this formula, and fortunately the 1995 English curriculum does little to prevent this.

On 30 September 1994 in the *TES* Lisa Jardine, Professor of English at Queen Mary and Westfield College, London University, published a splendid essay, 'Goodbye Little England', which should have been circulated to all members of SCAA. The essay summarises several of the main themes of this book. She describes how many Conservatives believe the best traditions of English are being undermined. In this model there is a precious object called English whose survival is threatened by a range of forces from without: popular culture, incorrect or non-standard usage, the media, foreign influences:

Crucially, arguments of this kind assume that the ideal to which they (and the education they advocate) aspire is fixed; that it does not change, but conforms to ideal patterns of language and expression defined at some unspecified moment in the historic past (probably the moment of Britain's greatest perceived imperial power towards the end of the 19th century). In these reside the civilised values which somehow we all continue to consider a humane education ought to provide. The question really is: Is it reasonable to ask for such cultural stability in a rapidly changing world? The Romans probably felt the same way about Latin. They succeeded in holding the line against outside influences on the language of Empire; and Latin no longer survives as a living language.

Lisa Jardine brings out why the Conservative take-over of the English curriculum endangered not only high standards of English in schools but also the whole future of literature by English writers. Young people today should be encouraged to read V.S. Naipaul, Derek Walcott, Alice Walker, Toni Morrison, Wole Soyinka, etc. Here is true vitality in new writing.

Yesterday morning I read Wordsworth's *Excursion*, just for pleasure because I have been re-reading works I have not looked at for many years. My wife and I have recently finished reading Maya Angelou's *I Know Why the Caged Bird Sings*. In the evening we opened a bottle of wine and played a video of the film, a work of high quality with a splendid performance by Constance Good as Maya. Enthusiasts for the Arts today have amazing resources at their command, from traditional classics to new world literature to great films. One of my daughters (aged 34) has just dropped in to return my copy of Toni Morrison's *Beloved*, which she has read with compassion and horror at its depiction of the treatment of slaves. During the last year we have all watched great films such as *The Age of Innocence, The Piano, Howards End* and *The Remains of the Day*. I have been arguing that the film of *Howards End* is a greater work of art than the novel, which has major flaws not in the film. (In the novel the sexual relations between Helen and Leonard are unbelievable.) My recent theatre visits range from Shakespeare's *Julius Caesar* at the Royal Exchange, Manchester, to a local production of Willy Russell's *Our Day Out* by a group of mostly young people, directed by my wife. Most days we watch some television.

English teachers with an enthusiasm for their subject could provide similar lists. The attempt to confine the school curriculum to an 'English' literary heritage comes mainly from people who do not participate in this artistic variety, and who often are bewildered and even frightened by multicultural events.

Lisa Jardine describes how she recently interviewed Wole Soyinka on Radio 3's arts magazine, *Nightwaves*:

> His view was that cultures have to decide whether they want to be broad and open to influences or narrow and inward looking. Whether their future is one of growth or of paralysed insularity will depend on that decision. 'Societies which open themselves out to other cultures are doing themselves a lot of good. Those who refuse to are merely curtailing their horizons. I do not consider myself a cultural evangelist, but I consider I was very fortunate in being introduced at an early age to other cultures and discovering through my own inquisitiveness the richness of other cultures.'

For Soyinka the receptiveness of one culture to another is a measure of its capacity to adapt to change. Britain stands at a cultural crossroads, and faces a choice. Either her literature can blossom and develop, nurtured both by writing in English from the past and from outside the British Isles, or it can look inwards and backwards to its literary past and fossilise. Teachers of English need to resist this fossilisation; the English National Curriculum of 1993 which reduced our culture to a nostalgic dream of the past was finally rejected by the combined efforts of hundreds of teachers. From 1995 onwards we need to develop programmes of study which celebrate all kinds of vitality in our national life, which arouse in children an enthusiasm for what is happening now in the Arts and for what may happen in the future.

Beverley Naidoo in 'The Territory of Literature: Defining the Coastline' (*English Education*, NATE, Spring 1994) commented on the absurdity of setting up definitive notions of English literature. If you are Irish you can produce Englishness: hence the inclusion in the NCC book lists of Swift, Yeats, Wilde, Shaw and Seamus Heaney; if you are Welsh, like Dylan Thomas or R. S. Thomas, you are supposed to be contributing to an English culture. Also in the English canon are Robert Burns and Jean Rhys, born in Dominica, the island in the Caribbean which became English after it was appropriated from the French, and Joseph Conrad, a Pole. These names make the exclusion of writers from India or Africa ridiculous. Beverley Naidoo writes:

> To read with one's students Conrad's *Heart of Darkness* and not to read Ngugi's *The River Between* or Achebe's *Things Fall Apart* is to deny students access to the voices of people on the banks of the river up which Conrad's colonial steamer sailed. Conrad's vision was limited to what he could view from its deck. Profoundly horrified by the contrast between the imperial idea and its actuality, he nevertheless could only hear a savage babble of sounds coming from the African river banks, thereby confirming Kurtz's vision. It is surely only after reading for themselves some original African fiction, that students can begin to be aware of the range of voices which Conrad could not supply.

To confine ourselves and our students to a narrowly determined literary heritage is to impoverish ourselves. In 1991 the Booker Prize was won by Ben Okri, a Nigerian. The short list included Timothy Mo, half-Cantonese, educated in Mill Hill; Rohinton Mistry, born in Bombay, then living in Toronto; William Trevor, an Irishman living in Devon; Roddy Doyle from Ireland; and Martin Amis, whose favourite authors are American and whose subject in *Time's Arrow* is the Holocaust. Vitality in literature in English in the 1990s is to be found on the margins, not at the centre (Salman Rushdie is a prime example). The chair of the Booker judges in 1991 was Jeremy Treglown, previously editor of the *Times Literary Supplement*, now Professor of English at Warwick University. He gave a spirited after-dinner speech (the long one, after the TV cameras have been turned off!) specifically defending the Cox Report against the growing attacks from Conservative nationalists:

❦ ...the report warned of what was known two hundred years ago to that most conservative of linguists, Samuel Johnson: that all languages, like all societies and their cultures, must change. As Johnson put it, 'sounds are too volatile and subtle for legal restraints; to enchain syllables, and to lash the wind, are equally the undertakings of pride, unwilling to measure its desires by its strength'.... It can sometimes seem as if literary people choose to hide in a Heritage theme-park, where, after the family has spent the evening around the piano, Father reads aloud to them from Trollope. There's no doubt that cultural ostrichism has its attractions, and some strengths. But it means missing so much.... No one even half-conscious who had recently looked around a British city could suppose that Bombay or a Nigerian village are settings less immediate to the imaginations of readers here than Barchester.

The extreme right-wing view is authoritarian, its aim to impose a national state identity on children in schools. The opposing view is democratic, to allow ethnic self-expression, to choose representative texts for study in the classroom which reflect a whole range of cultures, class, languages and gender.

Literary theory

In British and American universities a great debate has raged for many years about the status of literary theory. There have been turbulent confrontations over such changing critical fashions as structuralism, deconstruction, Marxist criticism, feminism, cultural materialism, new historicism and psychoanalysis. Such debates concern major issues over civil liberties, nationalism and its shortcomings, censorship, education and the media. Classrooms cannot be isolated from such debates. It is generally agreed by almost all university teachers today that the canon must not be restricted to DWEMs (dead, white European males); and that we must follow Wole Soyinka's advice to open our minds to other cultures. As I explained in chapter 2, the Cox Report argued that 'cultural analysis' should be an essential element in the English curriculum.

In the 1990s there have been a number of attacks on the way literary theory has come to dominate the syllabus, particularly in American universities. There are two main criticisms: first that study of theory now takes place with very little reading of literature itself, and second that students are being swamped with jargon as university teachers avid for promotion publish tomes of badly written prose.

Criticisms of the replacement of the reading of great literature by turgid literary theory have come in recent years from Harold Bloom's famous book, *The Western Canon* (1994), Louis Simpson's *The King my Father's Wreck* (1995) and numerous writings by Frank Kermode. Kermode quotes Hector in *Troilus and Cressida*: '*Tis mad idolatry to make the service greater than the god.*' Tom Paulin, a left-wing English poet, complained about the gobbledygook which has made many recent books on literary theory unreadable: '*Most theorists write like Flymo lawnmowers. They do not enjoy the English language*' (*TES*, 11 June 1993). In the mid-1990s there is a sense of exhaustion in the study of theory, and it could be that English teachers in schools can participate in the debate at a time when it is not too difficult to reject the jargon and the excesses, and to keep what is best. The study of literature has never ceased to be at the centre in school programmes of English, and there is no reason why this should not prevail in the future.

I believe that study of literature (and of media texts, as I shall argue below) must involve honest discussion about quality, must involve analysis and discrimination. Some books and films are better than others, and it is dishonest for teachers not to argue for their own point of view about values. This ought to be self-evident. In 'Is There a Critic in the House?' in the *Independent* on 25 January 1995, Malcolm Bradbury deplored the way in many universities the traditional liberal aims of raising standards and training taste have been largely replaced by analysis of culture as a phenomena: '... *the once separate realms of high and mass culture have come into equivalence; common texts, equal manifestations of the vast stylistic and expressive pluralism which is the post-modern spirit itself.*' Culture seems to be drifting progressively downmarket (as TV schedules make plain) and there is an urgent need for critics of an independent mind to oppose this trend. Bradbury thinks the blatant manipulation and commodified cliches of many television programmes and advertisements must be subject to serious criticism:

> The real reason for taking criticism seriously is the desire to take art seriously, as an exploration, an investigation, a fundamental probe into our moral, our spiritual and our imaginative life. That depends on a desire for standards, for judgment, for the endless sifting of the better from the worse.

I know many teachers of English share my wish to see this notion of criticism at the centre of English studies. As I describe these debates, so very briefly, I hope I make clear why a narrowly defined prescriptive national curriculum is so dangerous to the free play of the mind. Sometimes the Cox curriculum has been called a 'compromise'. I prefer to think that it leaves issues open for discussion in the classroom and for teachers to determine their own emphases.

Media studies

These arguments are especially relevant to media studies. I would not pretend to be sure how far more emphasis on media studies will be thought appropriate as we move into the next century. The issues need constant debate by teachers. In discussion of the Cox curriculum in *Critical Quarterly* (Winter 1990), Colin MacCabe wrote:

> The Cox Report's weakness on literature is not the result of its failure of conservative nerve to assert a common literary curriculum but its failure of radical nerve in following through the logic of the National Curriculum and placing media education as the counterpart to its insistence on the teaching of Standard English.

MacCabe's argument is that radio, film, video and television have become the popular culture, the one art form in a democratic society which unites us all, and therefore study of the media should be at the centre of the curriculum. I do not agree with him that in the 1990s we are ready for a great shift from reading of literature to study of media texts. I do believe that English teachers must not put their heads in the sand and that media studies must be part of the curriculum. In 'From Cultural Cleansing to a Common Curriculum' (*English and Media Magazine*, Summer 1993) Cary Bazalgette, Principal Education Officer at the British Film Institute, wrote:

> In reality, the media threaten to make English redundant. Literary adaptions are only a small part of this threat. It is the enormous overall creative, communicative and democratic potential of the media which demands that they are taken into account, if we really want to think about what a desirable curriculum might be for children starting school in the 21st century.

In courses on cultural studies the following question is often asked: '*What role should the study of literature play in a society that appears increasingly to marginalise print culture, where what is called great literature is only read with pleasure by a minority?*' Just as Latin and Greek were replaced by English literature at the centre of the curriculum, so are we now seeing an inevitable move where English literature will become a minority subject?

Cary Bazalgette attacked John Patten's attempt to stop this process by imposing a nationalistic English curriculum. She wrote of his proposals: '*Bathed in a rosy fin de siècle sunset, we can all forget about the horrid complexities of technology, multiculturalism and the media, and concentrate on the cosy certainties of grammar and the convivial fireside glow of Edwardian verse.*' Our national culture, she argued, '*goes on developing and changing through miscegenation and argument.*' The attempt of Patten and Pascall to invoke 'standards' which exist independently of playgrounds, streets and football matches, and in spite of television, films and video, is forlorn and impossible. She thinks English teachers are deluded if they view the main significance of media studies as their 'usefulness' for English, if they think that the value of soaps is only that they help us to study Dickens's use of the serial, or that the principal educational importance of seeing *Middlemarch* on TV is that pupils might be helped to read and enjoy the novel.

I agree that media studies must exist in their own right, but I do not believe that English literature is becoming a minority subject, nor that English will ever be redundant. The pleasure of reading is still a powerful force among children and young people. I acknowledge that these questions raised by Cary Bazalgette must not be closed down by a prescriptive curriculum.

I am surprised that some academics still deny that film can produce great art. As a young man my pleasure in seeing *La Strada, Les Jeux Interdits, City Lights* or *Bicycle Thieves*, among so many wonderful films, was in every way comparable to my excitement at watching great plays or reading great literature. And I have been overwhelmed by some television programmes, particularly documentaries. I think, however, it is unfortunate that some teachers of cultural and media studies do not discriminate between texts. I think that the experience of watching *Middlemarch* is superior to the experience of watching *Blind Date*, and if this is true for me as a teacher I ought to say so. As Cary Bazalgette herself argues, teachers need to help children to have high expectations of the media, to deal with issues critically, to empower them, just as we do in the study of literature, to appreciate what is best. This does not mean making them repeat our ideas hypocritically. It means open debate, and access in the classroom to what the teacher believes is of high quality. It means encouraging children to develop their imaginations.

Cary Bazalgette argues for a conceptual framework for a curriculum which includes both literary and media texts. Study of books and films should be asking the same questions: who is communicating with whom and why?; how has the text been produced and transmitted?; how does it convey its meaning? Both literary and media texts need to be deconstructed to examine the rhetorical techniques by which meanings are conveyed. She offers a conceptual framework based on narrative, audience and representation. Representation signals a way of thinking about texts which generates intriguing and challenging questions: how real is this text meant to be?; why does this text not use a natural chronology? In such programmes of study, texts from different sources can be studied side by side.

This conceptual framework needs to be discussed at teachers' conferences and when teachers are being trained. At this stage of the debate, questions have to be asked about how far teachers of English are prepared for this approach. Developments of this kind only succeed if they are supported by well-trained, enthusiastic teachers.

In this chapter I have not dealt specifically with drama or the craft of writing, because I have already emphasised their importance in earlier sections of this book. Suffice it to say that I wish to see both drama and the craft of writing accepted as essential components of all courses in English, from primary school to higher education.

Conclusion

Dangers of political interference

In this book I have described in detail a series of events which should not have occurred in a democratic society. From 1991 to 1995 a small group of Conservatives interfered with the National Curriculum in order to impose an extreme right-wing version of the knowledge and skills necessary for the education of our children. Opposition to the Conservative takeover of the National Curriculum came almost entirely from the teaching profession, helped particularly in 1993 by parents, not from the Labour Party.

In the late 1980s all the main political parties welcomed the idea of a national curriculum. After the Education Reform Act of 1988, which set up the framework for the National Curriculum, there was a considerable degree of consensus between professionals and politicians on the way forward, but this was broken in 1991.

In the 1990s everyone knows about the divisions in the Conservative Party about Europe. The divisions over education and the National Curriculum have been less publicised. In 1993 and 1994 when I addressed audiences of parents and teachers I often claimed that I represented the majority of Conservatives, and that John Patten spoke for a small minority. I met many Conservative councillors who were furious at the votes they were losing because of the mishandling of the National Curriculum. At the debate which opened the BFI Commission of Inquiry into English in November 1993, Sir Malcolm Thornton, Conservative MP for Crosby and Chairman of the Parliamentary Select Committee on Education, Science and the Arts since 1989, spoke for these disaffected Conservatives:

❻ It is also important to remember that the implementation of legislation is not done by politicians. It is done by practitioners. Politicians can pontificate as much as they like, but at the end of the day, it is the teacher or lecturer in front of his or her class who actually delivers those reforms. Unless those very people feel a strong sense of ownership of what they are doing - the ownership of the reforms, and ownership of the system - then I believe that the system is indeed in jeopardy, and so often of late that feeling of ownership has, in my view, been sadly lacking.... I personally am very unhappy about the belief that somehow market forces will solve all these problems. I cannot see that 24,000 schools, bobbing around like corks on a market sea, are going to have very much in the way of coherence or vision. (Report of the Commission of Inquiry into English, BFI, 1994, pp. 163-4)

I admire Sir Malcolm's courage in taking this stance. I believe that in the late 1990s his views will prevail.

The unfortunate events which took place after 1991 deserve close attention when policies for education for the future are debated. Here is a list:

◆ *The decision by Kenneth Clarke in 1991 to allow a small right-wing group to take over NCC and SEAC.* In chapter 2 I described Kenneth Baker's wish that NCC should be independent and respected by the teaching profession. I argued that SCAA should be independent and seen to be independent. Members should be appointed not by the Minister, but by a variety of independent institutions (head teachers' associations, for example, together with perhaps one person elected by the CBI and one by the TUC). If the Labour Party comes to power and creates an independent statutory General Teaching Council, this body might take over control of SCAA.

◆ *The decision by Tim Eggar and Kenneth Clarke in 1991 to censor the LINC materials on the English language.* £21 million had been spent on the LINC project! The teaching materials have gained a considerable international reputation. The decision to withdraw funding was made by politicians who knew little about the English language and who were looking for good media publicity.

◆ *The misuse of the Warwick research by NCC in the summer of 1992.* A pretence was made that radical revision of the English curriculum was necessitated by the discovery of major weaknesses by the unpublished Warwick research. This was a false claim. Research on education should not be kept secret, particularly when it affects important government decisions. At present, research belongs to the commissioning organisation, and is confidential. Both NCC and SCAA have delayed publication of research when the conclusions cast doubt on government policy. This should be made illegal.

◆ *The manipulation of the curriculum to serve political ends.* For example, in 1991 Kenneth Clarke decided on his own initiative that modern history, studied by children aged 14 to 16, should run from the turn of the century to a time 20 years before the present (see chapter 2).

◆ *The failure of John Patten to listen to teachers.* NCC was required to consult the teaching profession. The consultation process in summer 1993 of the revised English curriculum was a sham. The September 1993 version described the consultation process in a deliberately obscure fashion, and in fact retained most of the features condemned by the teaching profession.

◆ *The takeover of SEAC in 1991 by right-wingers with no professional knowledge of the complex problems of assessment.* In chapter 6 I described the secrecy with which policy decisions were taken, the pretence (again) of consultation with teachers, and the resultant muddles and confusions which damaged the education of thousands of children.

◆ *The decision by John Major, based on ignorance and prejudice, that coursework assessment for English should be drastically reduced.* The National Curriculum for English can be properly assessed only if it involves a considerable element of coursework assessment. The decision in 1995 to reject Sir Ron Dearing's proposal, that in the allocation of marks for English at GCSE coursework should be increased from 40 to 50 per cent, was taken against all professional advice and was damaging to teacher morale.

◆ *The attacks by John Major, based on ignorance and prejudice, on media studies.* Analysis of media texts should be an important element in the English curriculum, and is vital in a democratic society.

◆ *The waste of millions of pounds on curriculum revisions.* The revisions of the English curriculum were deplored by almost everyone in education with knowledge of modern research and modern developments in the teaching of English. The money could have been spent on school books.

◆ *The continual unjustified attacks by Conservatives on the teaching profession.* Teacher morale was undermined from 1991 onwards by sensational attacks on the competence of teachers as well as by the ill-considered revisions of the English curriculum. Teachers had worked hard to implement the 1989 curriculum. After 1991 their professional advice was ignored, and they had to cope with both administrative confusion and sudden shifts of policy. The restoration of teacher morale is a prime requirement for high standards in the future.

The future for the English Curriculum

I have already referred to the article on 3 March 1995 in the *TES* written by three professional officers from SCAA. This makes it clear that, after all the arguments and waste of money, teachers from 1995 onwards should continue to base their work on the programmes of study in the Cox curriculum, and that the 1995 English curriculum demands little change. The officers wrote:

> One important point to note is that although teachers will need to check their current planning against the revised Order, it is likely that, if teachers are currently teaching the full range of requirements, wholesale replanning of schemes of work will not be necessary. A second point is that the revised Order is to be taught according to teachers' professional judgments. There is no implied methodology and, as the general requirements state, no implied hierarchy or teaching sequence in the presentation of the Order. Third, the revised Order represents the minimum requirement; beyond this statutory entitlement, it is up to teachers to develop the English curriculum as they see fit.

This advice was followed up on 24 March in the *TES* by a letter from Sir Ron Dearing himself. He insisted that the new arrangements allowed increased discretion for schools over the depth of treatment of the content of the revised 1995 curriculum:

> There is no requirement to teach every specified topic at the same level of detail. It is for teachers to decide which elements to treat in depth and which in outline.
>
> Recognising that schools with inspection in prospect would be anxious about using such discretion, HM Chief Inspector of Schools joined me in writing a letter to all head teachers in November 1994 giving support for this approach.

These pronouncements make it clear that it may now be possible for teachers to reclaim the curriculum, and to teach according to good practice. The remaining large worry concerns the nature and significance of assessment in the future.

I conclude by listing ten features which should be at the centre of the post-1995 English curriculum:

◆ Teachers should use a variety of approaches in the teaching of reading. Teachers should develop appropriate classroom techniques, and keep abreast of the latest research.

◆ Pupils should be encouraged to write in a variety of forms, preparing drafts to be discussed with the teacher and their peers. They should write for real audiences, and on occasions their work should be published in class and school magazines. High standards in handwriting and spelling are a *sine qua non*.

◆ Teachers themselves should write, in whatever forms please them, and when appropriate show their work to their pupils. They should act as role models.

◆ There should be a strong commitment to drama in the classroom, and to high standards of speaking and listening.

◆ All pupils should be helped to speak and write Standard English by the age of 16.

◆ The LINC project should be revived and funded by Government. The Cox proposals for knowledge about language, including grammar and Standard English, should be reintroduced in the classroom and properly evaluated. The value of the linguistic and cultural knowledge of bilingual children should be recognised.

◆ Choice of texts for reading should keep to the framework in the Cox curriculum. Texts should be chosen from a variety of genres, from works from pre-1900 English literature, including Shakespeare, and from writings in English from other cultures. Teachers should be free to choose texts they and their pupils will enjoy.

◆ Media texts should be studied in the classroom.

◆ The requirements of children with special needs should be carefully evaluated by teachers and advisers with specialist knowledge.

◆ A significant element of the assessment of English should be by coursework.

For many years now there has been a consensus among good teachers about these proposals. The ideas about the teaching of English in the Bullock, Kingman and Cox Reports, and in the LINC project and Warwick research, can be seen as an organic growth. The events from 1991 to 1995 were malignant, and the patient has not yet been restored to full health. I urge teachers of English to be optimistic, to congratulate themselves on the campaigns of the last four years, and to continue the struggle for good practice in the teaching of English.

Select Bibliography

Abbs, Peter, *The Educational Imperative*, Falmer Press 1994.

Allen, David, English, *Whose English?*, National Association of Advisers in English 1988.

Bain, Richard *et al*, *Looking into Language*, Hodder and Stoughton 1992.

Bazalgette, Cary (ed), *Primary Media Education*, BFI Education Dept. 1989.

Bazalgette, Cary (ed), *Report of the Commission of Inquiry into English*, BFI 1994.

Black, Paul, *et al*, *Education: Putting the Record Straight*, Network Educational Press 1992.

Brindley, Susan (ed), *Teaching English*, Routledge 1994.

Brownjohn, Sandy, *To Rhyme or Not to Rhyme?*, Hodder and Stoughton 1994.

Carter, Ronald, *Knowledge about Language and the Curriculum: the LINC Reader*, Hodder and Stoughton 1992.

Cox, Brian, *Cox on Cox: An English Curriculum for the 1990s*, Hodder and Stoughton 1991.

Curriculum Council for Wales, *Review of National Curriculum English*, CCW 1993.

Crystal, D., *Who Cares about English Usage?*, Penguin 1985.

Crystal, D., *The English Language*, Penguin 1988.

Daugherty, Richard, *National Curriculum Assessment*, Falmer Press 1995.

Dearing, Ron, *The National Curriculum and its Assessment: An Interim Report*, NCC and SEAC July 1993.

Dearing, Ron, *The National Curriculum and its Assessment: Final Report*, SCAA December 1993.

Department of Education and Science [hereafter DES], *A Language for Life* [Bullock Report], HMSO 1975.

DES, *English from 5 to 16*, HMSO 1984.

DES, *Report of the Committee of Inquiry into the Teaching of English Language* [Kingman Report], HMSO 1988.

DES and the Welsh Office, *National Curriculum: Task Group on Assessment and Testing: A Report* [and three supplementary reports], HMSO 1987 and 1988.

DES and the Welsh Office, *English for ages 5 to 16* [The Cox Report], HMSO 1989.

Department for Education [hereafter DFE] and Welsh Office, *English for ages 5 to 16 (1993)*, HMSO April 1993.

DFE and the Welsh Office, *English Anthology KS3*, SEAC 1993.

DFE and the Welsh Office, *English in the National Curriculum*, HMSO 1995.

Doyle, Brian, *English and Englishness*, Routledge 1989.

Gannon, P., *Assessing Written Language*, Edward Arnold 1985.

Goswami, U., 'Phonological priming and orthographic analogies in reading', *Journal of Experimental Child Psychology*, 49.

Greenbaum, S., *The English Language Today*, Pergamon 1984.

Graham Duncan, with Tytler, David, *A Lesson for Us All: The Making of the National Curriculum*, Routledge 1993.

Hayhoe, Mike, and Parker, Stephen, *Reassessing Language and Literacy*, Open University Press 1992.

Hayhoe, Mike, and Parker, Stephen, *Who Owns English?*, Open University Press 1994.

Leach, Susan, *Shakespeare in the Classroom*, Open University Press 1992.

Marenbon, J., *English, Our English*, Centre for Policy Studies 1987.

Marsh, George, *Teaching through Poetry*, Hodder and Stoughton 1988.

NATE, 'Made Tongue-Tied by Authority': New Orders for English?, NATE 1992.

NCC, *National Curriculum English: The Case for Revising the Order*, NCC 1992.

NCC, *English in the National Curriculum*, NCC September 1993.

Perera, K., *Children's Writing and Reading: Analysing Classroom Language*, Blackwell 1984.

Quirk, R. *et al.*, *A Comprehensive Grammar of the English Language*, Longman 1985.

Quirk, R., and Stein, Gabriele, *English in Use*, Longman 1990.

Raban, B., Clark, U. and McIntyre, J., *Evaluation of the Implementation of English in the National Curriculum at Key Stages 1, 2 and 3 1991-1993* [The Warwick Report], SCAA 1994.

SCAA, *English in the National Curriculum*, SCAA May 1994.

Stubbs, M., *Educational Linguistics*, Blackwell 1986.

Tomlinson, Sally (ed), *Educational Reform*, Rivers Oram Press 1994.

Index